Love Dream

Lillian Bosnack

WESTBOW
PRESS*
A DIVISION OF THOMAS NELSON
& ZONDERVAN

WestBow Press books may be ordered through booksellers or by contacting:

WestBow Press
A Division of Thomas Nelson & Zondervan
1663 Liberty Drive
Bloomington, IN 47403
www.westbowpress.com
844-714-3454

Scripture taken from the King James Version of the Bible.

ISBN: 978-1-6642-3047-7 (sc)
ISBN: 978-1-6642-3048-4 (hc)
ISBN: 978-1-6642-3049-1 (e)

Library of Congress Control Number: 2021907239

Print information available on the last page.

WestBow Press rev. date: 08/26/2021

Our Chance Meeting

fter Frank died, I saw myself facing loneliness, depression, and anxiety. I suppose that, like any widow, I wanted to be held, cherished, and (yes, even at my age) romanced into oblivion. So when Bill came on the scene, I was ready to take on the new challenges of dating. I'm glad I was up to the task when I met this handsome man. My newfound connection with Bill was the most romantic relationship I could ever imagine. Right from the start I was floating on a cloud of infatuation like a schoolgirl.

It was during those first few days of this new and exciting time that I considered jotting notes to chronicle my feelings. From the very beginning, I promised myself that I'd be open—even raw—about what I felt: I'd make entries into this diary that would give every detail of this romance that made me feel young again. In order to do that properly, I have to set the stage of just what led up to my pink-cloud experience, so that when I read it in years to come, I'll be able to live it again and again. That's how good it's been. Good enough to want to live it at least a thousand more times.

My late husband, Frank, was gone, and I was alone. I was also on a spiritual search because of the tragic circumstances that had overtaken me. I wondered how all of it could be within the plan God had for my life. In fact, I often asked, *Where are you, God?* I received no response to my tearful pleas. I felt so empty and alone that I considered just ending it all. But I knew that was not the solution.

A few days before Bill and I met, I was on my treadmill, trying to work out my frustrations. I got a good sweat, and I also got frustrated by what I was reading in my Bible. I attempted to focus on my physical activity and allow my mind to go into idle.

I call my treadmill a walking machine because I don't run. I power walk, and that provides a good workout for someone my age. There's no stress on my hips, knees, ankles, or bottoms of my feet. My extralarge-print Bible sits on the built-in platform, so I can read the eighteen-point print while I walk. Normally the scriptures give me a sense of peace and security, but that morning's reading only added to my angst, and I was arguing with the apostle Paul. I was into First Corinthians when I came across chapter 7, verses 39 and 40, where Paul tells me that if a woman's husband dies, she is free to marry anyone she wants—*only in the Lord.* He goes on to say that he thinks a widow would be happier if she remained unwed. Really, Paul? I mean, *really?* If I took a survey of the mature women I know who lost their husbands and are now single, I'd venture to say nearly all of them would beg to differ.

I'm so glad that the great apostle adds that those remarks are just his opinion and not directly from the Lord, because I sure don't agree with him on this issue. Paul could never understand a woman's viewpoint on such matters unless God gave him special insight. I'm going to get real here and give the apostle Paul a lesson in womanhood. I'm going to write my true, deep-seated feelings. Even though I may not have the right to do this,

I feel so strongly about it that I need to address this issue head-on. I have to write from my heart. I believe every woman would agree.

Since I'm confronting the apostle Paul in this closet diary, I don't think anyone will read it until I'm in heaven. At that time the Lord will straighten out my thinking (or Paul's). Until then I'll write just how it feels to be a mature woman who is lonely.

Since my husband died from Alzheimer's disease, I have lived in a daily emotional void. Up to his death, I was busy handling everything he needed. I was a diligent caregiver—even changing his incontinence protection when he had an accident. Although I loved Frank dearly, changing an adult as I would a baby wasn't beyond revulsion. I was still fine with that and viewed it as part of honoring him in his inability to care for himself. But the dark cloud of seclusion closed in on me from sunup to sundown, and I wanted to die. In fact, after sundown I found myself in the fetal position in that lonely bed. I was angry with God and frustrated about all that had happened. Could the apostle Paul have even a modicum of understanding of what I've been through? Could he know the deep desires that I have concerning security, companionship, and emotional fulfillment? I mean, come on, I just want to be held. Paul certainly doesn't comprehend how the loving arms of the man I cherish feel around me when I'm upset and in need of comfort. God made all of us women on the emotional side of the equation. Practical men (like the apostle) just don't get it.

I trust I'm no different from any other woman—I'm driven by my feelings. We all want to have our emotions stroked into contentment like that of a purring cat.

I suddenly realized my first entry—where I talked about wanting to be held, cherished, and romanced into oblivion—was not as honest as I intended. I remember promising myself that I'd be completely candid. Yet right there, from that beginning declaration, I glossed over what I really feel. I said "romanced into oblivion," when what I really meant was to be made love to until my eyes crossed. That's as real as it gets. Yes, I'm a churchgoing, God-loving woman. I'm also as human as the next female. That means I have desires that need to be fulfilled. I want human love with all its nuances.

I guess it's because I'm one of millions of women in the world who is older and alone that makes me go on and complete my thoughts. Like the WWII hero Audie Murphy, I've been to hell and back.

Before my Frank died of Alzheimer's disease, that sweet man went through so much agony of mind and spirit that it nearly killed me to watch him fall away. Because of that, I've struggled to get past the years of tragedy brought on by that dreaded illness and on to the next chapter of my life.

Since Bill has emerged and I'm in this fresh relationship, it feels like I'm experiencing a new book in my life, not just a new chapter. It's not that I possess an inconsiderate attitude. I don't have such a callous mindset. In fact, I'm very aware of my vulnerability at this point and just how I might word these feelings I have. All I've done is come to grips with the fact that Frank and I had a wonderful life before Alzheimer's—then a life with Alzheimer's. Well, how do I say it and still display my compassion? I'll just say it was a life filled with bitterness. Why bitterness? Actually, my bitterness was toward God. At times I even shook my fist in His face and shouted my questions heavenward. All that happened when Frank was giving me such a hard time. He would begin a conversation, and I would respond, then he would go blank. I'd ask him to talk to me about what he was feeling. Still, no response. I'd give up and go into the kitchen to make supper. That's when he'd start to talk again. I'd stop what I was doing to go back to him sitting in the living room. "What were you saying?" I'd ask. He would be blank again. It was as though he was taunting me. He couldn't help it, but my emotions were on edge, and the frustration mounted.

But his death brought myriad mental upheavals, and I had difficulty coping with them all. As time is a healer, the weeks did alleviate many of the raw spots—even the bitterness left me, and I restored my relationship with my creator. What a relief that's been.

Now that Frank is gone and Bill is in the picture, a new set of emotions has surfaced. That's my problem. Since I've somewhat recovered from my loss of Frank, I'm trying desperately to sort out my thoughts about this new and intriguing man who has emerged like some kind of apparition of love. He's vastly different from Frank. He looks different and has a personality that is much more outgoing than Frank ever displayed. Bill can be ultra-serious at times and then turn on a dime to become extremely humorous. That aspect of his personality has my head spinning. At times I wonder when to take him seriously and when to see into his heart of hidden humor.

His name is William Harper Carrington. Since he prefers to be called plain old "Bill," that's what I call him. He's a wonderful cross between elegance and brawn. Maybe that's why I began this journal. Maybe God was leading me to write just after Frank died so I could use this diary to vent before I met Bill. And I have to admit, keeping this journal has helped me cope with my mental upheavals. From the beginning, I assumed these reflections might help me understand my emotional turmoil and give me more insight into my needs. When I write my true feelings and then read them, I have a much more objective view of myself. It's a true mirror of my real soul—like *the me* I've never seen in the light of reality. I can see my image in a mirror, but that same mirror can't allow me to see into my soul. However, as I read my in-depth journal notes, my soul seems to reflect the real me between the lines. I wonder if I'll continue to be as open as I have been now that Bill has come into my life. I'm getting quite deep, and I wonder if that will continue as my life lightens up with this newfound romance.

One thing's certain. I don't want to ever forget that I'm a Christian first, and everything else comes after that. However, Christians have feelings, desires, and even temptations. I guess I'm stepping into deep waters here. But I'm determined to write all that I am inside. It's got to come out, or I'll burst. It'll be a microscope into my soul, a very close look at who I am and why I feel the way I do.

Before jotting down my relationship with Bill, I want to scrutinize my life with Frank. And since Frank was so different from Bill (and Frank is gone), I need to recall who he was before his sickness—the real Frank. He was always loving and kind, even tender; one of the few men who enjoyed lengthy periods of snuggling. I needed that kind of man. However, my emotional needs stopped being met early into his disease. We even quit having any kind of loving, physical relationship at the onset of his mental breakdown. That was many years ago. The early development of Alzheimer's put him into a lethargic mode that kept him from expressing his feelings for me. He became a completely different man. Snuggling together went first. He no longer touched me. We lost connection. In fact, the disease made him almost manic-depressive. He was mostly depressed. Those times he was manic were born out of his frustration to remember anything at all.

As the months and years passed, he laughed a lot, and then he cried and slumped back into the cocoon of his depression. We only touched when he needed help with something. Once Alzheimer's had fully set in, Frank never reached out to hold my hand or give me a squeeze like he did so often before his illness.

Actually, before Alzheimer's took him away, we used to walk on the beach for hours, holding hands all the while. There's something very special about holding hands with the man who is the love of my life. The bond of togetherness is fortified as the tender grip of two hands joined in a love relationship continue through life's journey. I remember that there were times when his hand actually moved on mine in a secret way that was so sensual that I wanted to stop where we were on the lonely beach and offer myself to him with a deep kiss.

That was the time in our lives when Frank and I were at our best. Then the disease hit, and Frank's touch went by the wayside.

It's odd, but I didn't realize how much I had missed those masculine touches until Bill's first act of tenderness. Bill touched me so ... so ... oh, not intimately; but there was something in his initial touch that spoke to my soul. Something that was so deep and personal that it shook me to the core. When it happened, I wondered if I should feel such urges at my age. Now that I consider it, I'm certain that these sensations are part of humanity no matter what age. I remember how an intense breath heaved my chest and a chill ran up my spine. My entire body reacted to his soft caress. I could feel the sensation go through to my fingertips. Me! A mature woman being tantalized by the tender touch of a mature man. The thought of it takes me beyond my wildest dreams. And as I jot it down I'm experiencing the same warm feelings. As I recall it, the

7

feel of Bill's skin against mine is as tender and sweet as any sensation God ever created. And, oh, how his kisses make me young again. Of course, they bring memories of how Frank and I used to be when we were so very young and deeply in love. But with Bill it's a new adventure. Here's a man who can make my world spin out of control. I'll have to admit, to my recall Frank never made my heart flutter the way Bill does.

I just sat back and read that last line and asked myself if that really is true. Does Bill rock my world that much? Do I now have a warped sense of these two relationships? Did the young woman who met Frank so many years ago mature into an older woman who has a very different take on what thrills her?

As I try to picture scenes with Frank when we first met—I was well established in the business world and so was he—I wonder if we were jaded toward too much affectionate display. Wow! That thought knocks me back for a second look. I hope that wasn't the case. If it was, I sure missed out on some great demonstrations of love that Bill now provides.

I have to stop right here. I'm getting off into dreamland before I pen just how my relationship with Bill began and where this all plays out in the Lord's plans for my life. If I'm going to put it all in perspective from these hodgepodge journal notes I'll have to go back to the first instance—that flash in time when we met. It was an electrifying moment that changed the course of history for me. It was an explosive transition that reversed the agony of Alzheimer's. The entire episode turned into ecstasy for this enduring caregiver. It happened in an instant, as though God said, "I'm proud of the way you hung in there with Frank. Now, I'm going to reward you with Bill."

Am I dreaming or what?

Anyway, here's what actually happened. Not long after Frank died, I attended a caregiver's survivor's class in Clearwater, Florida. Those attending were people who were hurting, lost, lonely individuals—mostly made up of grieving spouses like me. It was one of those group functions that allow each person to vent and grieve openly to those who understand, because they're grieving too. It's a great opportunity to let out all the pent-up emotion. All of us had experienced the emotional rollercoaster ride through months or years or decades of giving and never receiving. Now that we have fulfilled our promise for better or worse, we're into a whole new phase of life—unfamiliar territory, to be certain.

From my seat near the end of the seventh row, I scanned the crowd. I could sense that everyone in that room was hurting. My gaze went from one to the others, and each had that same shroud of despair. Empty eyes were clouded with the feeling that life held no hope, no happiness, and no companionship. I wondered how any of us would be able to enjoy even a modicum of contentment now that our lives had been so shattered. Would we ever be able gather up the shards and glue life back together? It was a toss-up between calling our deceased mates back from the grave and unsuccessfully trying to go on with this empty existence while looking for a new companion.

I left that first meeting without answers but not without expectation. From moment to moment, I vacillated from the mountaintop of hope to the dark valley of desolation. Within days I returned and took my same chair for a second meeting with those despairing souls. It was always gloom and doom. No one had a smidgen of joy. I listened and slumped with them. Yet under all that misery I felt something fantastic was right around the corner for me. It was just a flicker of hope. Attending that second meeting was simply another attempt to find solace for my grieving heart. It wasn't much different from the first meeting. Again, I left the room hurting and still grieving. I even considered that I too should let go and die. I cringed. My hopes and dreams were all in the very distant past. I dealt with Frank's Alzheimer's disease for so long that I've forgotten exactly when the onset took place. As I consider it, during that survivor's meeting I didn't care. Oh, I loved Frank, and we had given those solemn vows—*for better or for worse, in sickness and in health*—and I kept them. With Alzheimer's there is no *better*. In the evolution of it all our roles reversed, and it wasn't enjoyable. I had to do everything for my once doting husband. As the days slogged by, Frank grew progressively worse. There were some good days, but most were nearly unbearable.

Later that week I went to the survivor's meeting for the third time; same seat, with the same empty looks on sagging faces. There were several new faces; also sagging, blurry-eyed and empty. It was quite crowded. In fact, I noticed that the seat next to me at the end of the row was the only empty one. Why I gave going to that meeting another attempt is beyond me. But now that I consider it, I feel like I had divine direction. At least that's my reasoning.

I suppose the reason I attended was more to get out of the empty house and away from the memories that lingered there. Too, loneliness draped its ugly arms around our home. Funny, but I can't seem to get used to the idea that it isn't *our* home any longer, but *my* home now. Even so, going to that meeting so depressed me that as others gave their sad stories there were times when I truly did want to die with them.

For some reason, before the meeting began that third night, I focused on a mental picture of a dear friend from the past. She and her husband, Joe, were getting ready to celebrate their fiftieth wedding anniversary when Joe was killed in a terrible accident. At his funeral she moved like a zombie. The horrific news of his instant death made her appear to have been hit on the head with a powerful sledge hammer that sapped all the life out of her. I compared her experience with mine. Instead of being hit by a mighty, single blow, Alzheimer's had slowly beaten me down. In place of a sledge hammer it was more like the constant taps of a ballpeen hammer, one tiny ping at a time, until my energy and zest for life slowly and methodically ebbed into nothingness.

It all makes me take a second look at myself to see if I've really become that cynical. I hate the idea of such a warped look at life. But I'll have to admit that it seems my tenderness for the plight of others isn't what it should be. I guess if any of my friends read this, they'd think I was far from the godly woman I profess to be. The reason I'm a bit jaded is because these meetings are depressing. Listening to people who hurt and are lonely, just like me, only adds depth to my darkened mood.

As I scanned the room that third night, my mind changed from depression to thankfulness. I was so lonely that, when I walked in and was accosted by one of the staff people, I stopped to listen. She presented the opportunity to get out of the house and actually do something beneficial for other people. She made a great presentation, so I signed up to volunteer my services. I was thankful to be among those who would empathize with me, should I choose to vent. But openly venting is not me. I'm not one to express my deepest feelings publicly. Why then did I sign up as a volunteer? It didn't make sense, but she convinced me that I have what it takes to counsel others into better mental health and emotional healing. Even so, my Bible tells me that when I'm at my weakest, God is strongest. I'll go with that by faith. But I feel in a turmoil myself, so helping others seems absurd. That's been true of my life lately; it doesn't make sense. But I feel like I have to flow with it. I'm experiencing divine direction like never before. It's a wild ride, but I can't get off at any point. I'm like a human robot, and God has total control. Seeing myself follow some sort of predesigned pattern is unnerving. I also feel secure in the hands of my Creator. Exciting? Yes. Odd? Yes. Nevertheless, contentment blankets me, and I'm filled with anticipation. My mind continually races to Jeremiah 29:11, and I see that the Almighty has a plan for me, but I'm just not sure what it is. It's intriguing in a way.

As I sat in that third meeting, I wrestled with the jumble of thoughts racing through my mind. The room slowly filled with grieving people. Why I kept coming back was determined by the fact that I was sad and depressed, and I looked for relief. That, I assumed, was the reason all of us were there. Yet, again I sensed that divine direction. That made the difference.

I scanned the crowd, sighed, and sat back to wait for the meeting to begin. Just as it was ready to commence, I noted that all the seats were taken except the one at my left elbow; an end-of-row seat. I furtively eyed the woman on my right. She appeared disheveled and defeated. She looked as if life had gotten the best of her. Or, I wondered, *was it death that did her in?* We didn't speak. She seemed shy, and I wasn't in the mood to begin a conversation, especially one where I had to carry the ball all by myself. I could do that to the mirror. I could feel a smile tug at my lips as I secretly thought, *I have done that to the mirror.* This woman carried misery and death on her shoulders. I'd had enough of that. I didn't need more of the same from people who were highly emotional and sensitive. A few more moments passed, and everyone hushed. The silence that permeated the room presented quite a contrast to business meetings I've attended where light conversation was the norm. I sighed again and resigned myself to another night of ache so deep that it would give me a migraine. I wished the meeting would get started so that it could come to a conclusion. My watch told me it was two minutes to seven. For some reason I stared at the face of it and let the second hand lull me into emptiness. Someone up front cleared her throat and I glanced up, aware of my surroundings once again.

That's when the door on the side wall opened for the last time. The moment he entered I noticed his silver hair, his very manly nose, and those sparkling blue eyes. Was I imagining it, or was a shaft of bright light emanating from this handsome man cutting through the grey haze of despair? To this day I'm not fully convinced either way.

After scanning the group for a place to sit he smiled at me. I glanced down at the only available chair on my left and moved my elbow in closer to my side so as not to make him feel I was saving it for someone. When I peered up and saw him coming my way, I offered a soft smile and slight nod then turned my eyes toward the front.

I'll never forget that spring evening, or the place—a hospice grief counseling group meeting in Clearwater, Florida. It was one of those transforming moments in which, from then on, life is never the same. It's a day from which fond memories are gleaned. And, oh, I am gleaning them.

Our Connection

ntil he walked through that door, I was convinced that all of us, every single person in the room, was doomed to bear the rest of life under a dark cloud. Only death would end our misery.

Had I known what would happen after that evening, I wouldn't have done anything differently. In the weeks and months following that initial meeting, Bill escorted me to heaven itself. The cloud I was floating on whisked me into bliss, and I was in love again. This love was more romantic, more passionate, and more appealing than anything I have ever dreamed could exist for me. That's not disrespectful toward my late husband. Frank was good. But Frank wasn't Bill by a long shot.

OK, I have to be very honest with myself. Yes, I do understand that a time of grieving can also be a time of vulnerability. And, of course, I understand that it can put rose-colored glasses on my darkened life to give me splashes of sunshine, twinkling lights, and dashes of dreams yet unfulfilled. I also realize that Christians sometimes distort biblical verses to fit their needs. But I'll forgo any and all rational thinking in order to experience what Bill and I are living—experience that prompted me to keep going with this journal.

Oops! There I go, getting ahead of myself. I want to

remember this the way it really happened, so I'll go back to our first encounter and make everything clear. My priorities are to remember just how this all unfolded. But my more conservative side is concerned that I'll be judged harshly. If anyone reads this when I'm gone, I want them to realize what transpired to bring Bill and me to where we are today. Their harsh judgment is a real concern for me. Maybe that's why I want to please God so much. He's the great judge. I don't want to stand before the Lord and hear that I've displeased Him. I've just experienced a huge sigh. It's time to get back to my recall of the third meeting.

As I sat in that room filled with Alzheimer's survivors, despair, drudgery, and disappointment were the sharp rocks leading down the rugged path of my future. Yet when that handsome man came up to me, gestured to the chair and asked, "Is this seat reserved for anyone?" his voice was a crisp, melodic baritone that shook me to the core. I could envision the sharp rocks morphing into lily pads of life spread across a pristine pond. Those soft green pads were my new steps to a magical transformation.

I felt giddy and uncharacteristically said, "Yes. I reserved it." He didn't flinch in the next silent moment, and I was in a bubble of sunshine in the middle of that dismal room. I snapped out of it and added, "I reserved it just for you." I tilted my head in a girlish, coy way. A sudden pang of regret for such a childish comment was quickly nullified by his warm smile. His teeth weren't perfect, but his smile was gorgeous. That smile glowed with confidence and a hidden sense of humor. His eyes sparkled with the light of life. He was not at this grief counseling meeting to reenact the death experience and all that led up to it. I sensed that he came to bring life. Maybe he was a volunteer who came to spread the joy of knowing there was a bright future ahead for anyone who would put the past in the past and leave it there. Then it struck me. A sudden knowing made me feel he had come to this meeting just to find me and to bring me the richness of his energy, his love of breathing the fresh, warm Florida air, and a new chapter in my life.

Immediately my mind raced into prayer mode.

Lord, did you send this man to me? I'm thinking that he can add so much to my life. But what do I have to offer him in return? Lord, please lead me. Keep me from saying anything that might ruin this thing from the start.

I didn't know what to call the moment, so I just referred to it as "this thing." Although I didn't realize what was ahead, now that I look back on it I think it would have been more appropriate if I'd said "this fling."

He took his seat next to me and I felt his hand brush mine. A tingle gave my body an unexplained rush from head to toe.

What's going on? I just read what I wrote and it sounds like something a teenager would put in her secret little diary tucked under her mattress. I'm not a teenager. I'm a mature woman. Maybe that's the problem. I'm too mature. That phrase people use about reverting back to childhood may be happening to me. Or possibly I'm having a reaction because of my freedom. I have to face the fact that I was shackled to Frank day and night for those fifteen long years of his sickness. I wonder if this new sense of independence has me in some sort of dream world. I can't remember exactly how the fourteen-year-old girl who lives across the street says it, but it goes something like, *It is just not me.* No, that isn't it. But it's true. Acting like this is just not me. Oh, I remember what she would say in this situation. *It's sooo not me.* Yes, that's how she would say it. And I agree.

Another thing that's different is that I'm writing this

in a journal. Why? I've never kept a journal—well, not since I was sixteen. This is very odd. Yet I'm compelled to keep going. Here's what I remember thinking about this man at the moment his hand touched mine.

The soft smell of his freshly scrubbed hair was like the scent of manliness, yet there was a hint of some fruity shampoo. The combination was heady. My throat was dry and I tried to swallow and catch a glimpse of his profile out of the corner of my eye.

He must have noticed that I was uneasy, because he asked, "May I get something for you from the refreshment table?"

"No! Ah, I mean, no thank you," I declined. "I'm fine."

He cocked his head and gave me *that look*. "Indeed, you are," he whispered.

I must have had a questioning frown because he followed it with a lifted eyebrow and added, "Fine."

I didn't know how to respond, or whether to respond at all. He was openly flirting with me. I looked down into my lap and fiddled with my fingers. Out of the corner of my eye I noticed that he had looked away and I raised my head to see what had his attention. He was scanning the room with no apparent object in his focus. He took a deep breath and leaned back just as the moderator opened the meeting.

Again, I sneaked a look at his profile and attempted to estimate his age. He appeared to be strong and rugged, but there was also something about him that appealed to my concept of sensitivity. I couldn't determine if he was a retired longshoreman who had labored hard to make ends meet or a man of means who never put in a day of hard work in his life. The amalgamation of his powerful good looks mingled with the elegant way he carried himself gave me much to ponder. It also made me determined to discover just who this man was and where he had come from. A deep breath of resolve raised my shoulders, and as I let it out, I relaxed.

We sat through some interesting dialogue by several people who were still raw from the wounds of their losses. Neither he nor I added anything to the overall discussions. And even though we didn't speak to each other we communicated through several glances—a wink by him, and a demure smile by me. It was as intoxicating as a bubbling glass of fine champagne, enhanced by soft lighting and carried along with musical strings. I was in heaven, and this handsome man was my knight in shining armor.

Even with the minutes ticking by I had no consciousness of the time. I was enthralled with the energy sitting next to me. A couple of sneaky peeks allowed me to realize that he was several years older than me in physical age, but I sensed that he was younger in disposition. In fact, I thought he was mentally and emotionally the youngest of the oldsters in the room. He was animated, enthusiastic, and exuded a wealth of energy. I wonder how I could have concluded all that about Bill before I knew his name? Even so, there was something about him that exuded that "It!" factor. He had star quality. I'm laughing because the stars were just in my eyes. His silver-grey hair was thinning just above the temples, but that only added to the intrigue of his aura. He appeared to be a man of breeding, but somehow a worldly sort as well. Again, I was captivated with the blend. In all my years I couldn't recall ever meeting a man who captured me in an instant like he did. I had heard of those who say they experienced love at first sight, but I never believed it was possible. Oh, I'm not saying I was instantly in love with this stranger. I'm saying the intrigue of the man himself was so overwhelming that

I was bordering on schoolgirl infatuation just by furtively eyeing him.

After the hour-long meeting he introduced himself. I'll admit I was cautious. I've heard about people who prey on those who have recently lost a loved one and I wasn't going to get scammed by some fancy pants wanting what I wasn't willing to give.

My worries were unfounded. From the beginning Bill was kind. When I gave him my name he repeated, "Lilly." He smiled. "A beautiful flower. A lovely name. And a very attractive lady." His gaze penetrated my soul and he added, "Your name makes me picture a small pond in the warmth of spring with lilies in clusters near the bank." He broke his trance-like stare to focus on the rest of my face. "And the two of us seated on a blanket of lush green grass, leaning against a large oak with a brook babbling to the songs of several birds flitting about."

I gasped. "You're a poet or novelist!"

He denied it and said, "My son's the writer in the family." Then he didn't hesitate and tossed the conversation ball to me. "And your children?" he ventured. I told him I never had children. Then we lobbed the verbal ball back and forth with ease. It was an intriguing experience in word dancing that lasted for nearly ten minutes. In that short time, we seemed to meld into a couple.

Am I dreaming? Why would I write that in this diary?
Did I really feel we were a couple at the moment? Was I that connected to this man I had only known a few minutes? Or, am I so smitten while entering my thoughts into this journal that I'm imagining that we were instantly joined at the heart? Is that what I was feeling *then* or is that what I'm feeling now that I've gotten to know him— really know him?

Making quick connections with men I've only

known a short time isn't within my genetic structure, my upbringing, or my character. I've always assumed that I'm a very practical thinking woman, even an old-fashioned type. I was a model in New York many, many years ago, working exclusively for Surrey Modeling, Ltd. After maturing beyond the youthful look the industry demanded, I took a position as an executive secretary for the law offices of Boston, West, and Hillbright. Both Manhattan firms were on *the list*. That's how they put it back in those days. It would be equivalent to being one of the *Fortune* 500 companies today.

When I retired, Frank sold his accounting practice, and we did the logical thing: we moved to the beach in Florida. I'm so practical that a fling at my age is about as far from who I am as New York is from Florida. That's why I have to sort out my thoughts. Bill and I aren't kids. We're practical thinking adults, and we don't jump off the deep end. Yet in that short encounter at the hospice meeting we exchanged names and phone numbers. And when we said farewell there was something in his eyes that compelled me to swallow hard. I could almost taste his sweet words as we lingered and stared at each other for the longest moment in recorded history. Then it was goodbye, and he was gone. A strange sense of loneliness enfolded me right there in that room, and I wanted to chase after him. Again, it was an impractical thing for me to do, or even to feel. However, the urge was there, and I couldn't deny it. He disappeared through the door, and I wanted to run after him and call out his name as I ran. The little girl in me was struggling to be free to do whatever she wanted. I yearned to grab his arm and hang on until... until what? Am I even able to think beyond that instant? As I'm writing this, I'm in a daze of recall. From that moment to this, Bill has kept me intoxicated with this love dream. I'm trying to be totally open and honest, but I find myself dreaming of how I hope it will be rather than exactly how it is.

Lord, please help me put this in my journal as it really happens. And for that which has taken place, let me recall it with clarity and truthfulness. Thank you Lord.

In the crowd that remained, one older woman came up to me. "Is that your gentleman friend?" she asked. She was overweight, wore too much makeup, and reeked of some awful sweet perfume.

I got coy. "Who?" I asked.

"That handsome man you were talking with a moment ago."

"Oh, Bill?" I laughed and lifted an eyebrow. "Can't you tell?" I chortled. As I turned to go, I winked at her. I only glanced back as I stepped through the doorway. She wore a frown of consternation pulling at her powdered brow. Oh, these feminine ways we women have. Sometimes I feel naughty for using the wiles God gave me.

In the hallway I ran into the disheveled woman who had been seated on my right. I nodded and was instantly sorry I did because she grabbed the moment. "May I talk with you?"

I was shocked. Everything in me tried to be sweet and cordial. My voice lifted. "Yes, of course," I said.

She stood only inches from me, and a slow smile played on her lips. "If you don't want him, I'll take him." Her smile widened and her brow lifted in anticipation.

I was shocked for the second time. "What?" I asked.

"That man," she said. "I'd love to have a man like that."

She wasn't at all the beaten down, grieving widow I'd imagined. She was on the hunt, and Bill was in her sights. I tilted my head to the right and said, "Bill and I ... well, you understand. He's taken."

Her brow rose. "Oh, I thought you just met him." She shrugged. "Can't fault a girl for trying." With that, she turned away.

I watched her subtle hip swing. It was a message to me that she didn't care anyway. A toss of her long auburn dye job and she disappeared through the door. I hoped she wasn't going to try to catch up with Bill. I immediately dismissed the notion and muttered. "He wouldn't have her."

I realize that people think and do strange things when they're emotionally destroyed. And right now, I'm thinking some very strange things. I just hope I don't do anything that's so strange that my friends will have me committed.

It was late the second evening after I met Bill. I was alone with my thoughts. Just after ten o'clock, I sauntered to the bedroom. Kitty, the striped tabby I brought home to soothe Frank during his emotional upheavals, was curled up on the spread at the foot of the bed. I absently reached down and patted her head. My day had been filled with things to do, but I didn't accomplish one of the items on the list; yet I was tired. I plopped down. Kitty stood, arched her back and leaned against me. She is such a loving cat. Wherever I am she presses against me. I can't even go to the bathroom without her arching her back and rubbing along my legs. She wants my attention all the time. I know how she feels.

While sitting on the side of the bed, I thought about the many years since Frank started his slip into Alzheimer's, and with it his touches, his caresses, and his love all disappeared. I ached, no, *longed for*, no, *yearned for* … Oh, I can't find the exact word for how deep the craving was, and still is, to be loved, cared for, and held as closely as possible.

I'm sitting here wondering if other women delve into deep fantasies like this. Do we all carry a child-like dream of love that may be only storybook fairytales? Are we prone to peek beyond the fog of life and see a new world where love and affection reign? Is that what all women do, or is it simply my slide toward immaturity—reverting back to childhood—that has me in a spin? I don't care. There, I've said it. I don't care what has caused this beautiful dream to invade my private thoughts, I'm going to go with it and quit trying to figure it out. That practical side of me will just have to suffer. I'm going with my desires, and that's that.

This Galahad who appeared out of nowhere seems to be the dream I've carried around in my mind for all these years. Even though Frank was unable to express love in any fashion, I still didn't want to be unfaithful to him. It was just that my humanness arose from time to time, and I wanted that expression acted out in tender touches, sweet whispers, and those loving looks that convey the most romantic affection. In fact, I'll admit that it became my deepest desire to find a man like Bill when Frank was deteriorating beyond recovery. I was so distraught that I wanted someone who would sweep me away on a great white horse, into a fantasy of my own making. I watched the reruns of *Pretty Woman* so many times I knew every line by heart. Like Vivian Ward, played by Julia Roberts, I admit that it's a fantasy of my own making, and I'm going to live it. The ache to be loved overwhelms me at times. And now I want to take my acquaintance with Bill further, just to satisfy my mind and determine what my future holds. But I have to be careful because he's a real man and … well, we all know what real men find fulfilling.

For years I cared for Frank and all the while loved him and looked after him. Yet there was a sense that when it was over, when God called Frank home, my opportunity for happiness would again present itself. I had no idea just how it would happen, but at times I knew deep in my soul that it would take place. Of course, there were many times I questioned my own rationality. It was a constant feeling of being on an emotional elevator. When those times of irrational thinking hit, I sank into depression. I went from floor to floor on that inner-elevator of my soul. That was especially true when I attended that first hospice grief counseling meeting. I vacillated when the raw nerve of my loss saturated my consciousness. I continually questioned what was going on with me after Frank died. Was God really going to bring love and affection back into my life? Or was I simply dwelling on a fantasy that would never find fulfillment? I fought against my negative thoughts, but I'll admit there were times when I felt totally defeated. I tried not to succumb, yet this devastating sense of uselessness and hopelessness permeated the very air I breathed. I truly wanted to be the overcomer our minister spoke of in his "Victory Series." When I attended our pastor's teachings, I got pumped up and ready to go out into the world and conquer those Goliaths that kept me bound to negativity. Too often, though, I'd slip back into depression, low self-esteem, and total lack of confidence.

Then I'd go back to church and sing those wonderful choruses that spoke of victory in our spiritual battles, and I'd be pumped again. In fact, Sunday's joyous time with my fellow Christians lasted all through Monday and sometimes into Tuesday. But slowly I'd ease back into the doldrums of everyday life at its worst. I fought a constant war. I wondered if I'd become manic-depressive too.

Before I put my head on the pillow, I asked God to reveal His will to me. I silently prayed.

Father, I have no idea what lies ahead, but You have my

*every breath in the palm of Your hand. Please lead me into
Your will for my life. I mean, I understand Your promises
found in Your Word, and that even my will plays a part in
all this. But I don't trust myself. I'm too emotionally raw
right now. So, I'm looking to You for answers. And Father,
if Bill is to be an integral part of Your plan for me, please
show that to me.*

After praying I opened my eyes. The glow of the night
light presented a haze, and my eyes wouldn't close. Kitty
pushed against my legs and curled up. I went over every
minute detail of the evening of my dreams. The picture
of Bill entering the grief counseling room ran over in my
mind at least a dozen times. My recall was sharper as I
allowed my eyelids to become heavy and drift into that
foggy state just before dropping off to sleep. His smile was
the last picture before morning awakened me.

I blinked as the sun peeked into the window. "Good
morning, Lord. Thank you for another day filled with a
future and a hope."

Kitty was right there by my knees. It seemed she hadn't
moved all night. I was so thankful for her companionship.
This was a new day, and I was ready to make it the best
day for my brightest outlook. I determined to be positive all
the way. I was brushing my teeth when I stopped to look
at my mature face in the mirror. My hair was a mess, and
I appeared older than my years. I grimaced at the image
staring back at me. "He wouldn't want an old lady like
you," I drawled. Jerking away from my expression, I spit
out the toothpaste and rinsed my mouth. After checking
my mirror image again, I came to a conclusion and spoke
bluntly as I stared at my reflection. "You're not getting

any younger, old girl." I squinted at myself. "If you're going after him, you'd better spruce up and look your best." I turned away and then, as an afterthought, I glanced back over my shoulder. "And you'd better hurry. Time is of the essence." I sighed and left the bathroom to encounter Kitty lying near the door. She got up and followed me into the kitchen.

Our First Phone Call

y morning cup of coffee is always something I cherish. Flavored coffee appeals to me. French vanilla is my favorite. As I leaned on the kitchen counter, I saw Bill's number lying next to the landline phone. In the three days since we met, I had touched it at least fifty times. Actually, the day after our meeting I picked up the handset to call him and then put it back in the cradle. A mental argument with myself ensued.

I'm from the old school. A decent woman doesn't make the initial move.

Then I changed to the other side of the argument. It wasn't easy to see that side.

But this is the twenty-first century, and women are free to do what they please. Having a date with Bill sure would please me.

My old nature kicked in, and I cast the rationalization aside. My roots in the church and the guidance created by my particular social understanding were too deeply ingrained. I couldn't make the first move. "Lord, if You're in this mess, please have Bill call me." I stared at the phone as though somehow willing it to ring. It didn't.

I went out onto the patio to lie back on the chaise lounge, sip the hot liquid, and daydream. The coffee was extra good, and Kitty jumped up onto my lap to curl up.

The smile I could feel stretching my lips made me come to a realization. "That's what I need too," I told her, "a lap to curl up on." She didn't respond. I nurtured the French vanilla flavor and mused about the possibilities of a future with Bill. I spent a good hour just toying with various scenarios. Why do we women do that? It seems that the entire feminine species will make something out of nothing. I rationalized that this casual nod from a man I'd never seen before and may never see again meant nothing. Yet here I was, making those storybook scenes come to mind. Not only did I daydream about him, I nurtured them into a mental book with page after page of affectionate hugs, playful antics, and tender kisses. I remember grunting at the thoughts. I was sure he wasn't sitting by the phone making a big deal about whether to call me or not. He's probably spent these few days doing what men do, fish with their buddies, or play golf, or ... I didn't want to think about him wooing another woman. I quickly dismissed that thought and considered what it would be like to have a man like Bill to wake up to. My fantasy moved to us sitting there on the patio as we ate breakfast together.

There I go with that Disneyworld dreaming again. I'm not Cinderella. I just smiled at my thoughts of Bill looking like a Prince Charming or Sir Galahad to me. I guess we all fantasize about love. However, I needed to face reality. Finally, I shook the dreams out of my mind and determined to face the day with the resolve to get done what needed to be accomplished—casting the love dream out of my mind. I figured that's all I could do. The phone wasn't ringing off the hook, and I wasn't about to call him. The flash thought ran through my mind as I wished I had given him my cell number just so I could be ready for a call if I were away from the house.

In order to deal with my emotions, I opted to put on clam diggers, a loose-fitting, scruffy top and my worn-out deck shoes to go out into the warm Florida air and work around my flower beds. I figured that would busy me enough to get through the day without Bill's image constantly invading my mind. Just in case God chose to answer my prayer quickly I took the satellite phone out to the open garage. After putting it on the work bench where I could hear it from the yard, I propped it up against a cardboard box and made certain the ringtone was set at its highest volume. Now that I look back on all that, I can only see the little girl in me. I've never been concerned about having my phone ring. If someone called and I didn't catch it, I'd get it later if they left a message. But this was different. I desperately wanted to hear Bill's greeting so that I could respond. If I missed his call, it would be an emotional disaster. At that moment I didn't realize how possessed I was; nor did I understand my deepest desire for affection. I wanted to be hugged and loved. The image was overwhelming me.

I sank into the work of gardening as best I could. The beds were beautiful, filled with floral perfection. God's wonderful paintings on each petal, the reds, blues, yellows, and every other color a person could imagine, dazzled me. My favorite flowers have always been my amaryllis blooms. Their trumpet shaped blossoms of variegated shades intrigue me. They seem to be one of God's ultimate creations, especially the pink ones. I also love to have plenty of lantana because of their delicate little blooms that remind me of a wedding wreath caressing a bride's brow.

Wait a minute! Do I have marriage on my mind already? I don't even know this guy!

I shook the thought and scanned the entire yard to clear

my thinking. I looked over the array of plants and sensed God's hand on my life. He has blessed me abundantly.

I have palms, azaleas, and tea olive trees. My gaze took in the beauty of each of God's wonderful creations. I'm so thankful that I have a real relationship with the Creator of all this.

Even so, due to Eve's encounter with the serpent, there was work to do. It wasn't just a bed of roses. There were thorns and weeds, and those pesky gnats to deal with all the time. I was thankful that love bug season had just ended and I didn't have to worry about them.

As I bent to pull up a few stray weeds trying to make their way up through the cedar-chip groundcover, I noted the pansies. Each little face smiled up at me. Their wide black eyes seemed to be amazed at the glow I emanated. At least I felt like I was glowing. My fingers cuddled one of the yellow faces, and I said, "Good morning, sunshine. Isn't it a wonderful morning?" It didn't bother me to talk to my plants. I did it often and even sang to them at times. I released the petals and allowed my eyes to sweep over the bed. "You girls aren't the only ones who are happy today." My gloved hands worked around the fragile little flowers. As I snipped off brown growth and pulled weeds, I forced my mind to focus on the chore at hand. "I'm going to make life better for all of you," I promised. My trowel got really busy. I turned on a mist of spray over the entire array of beds, and within the hour they all took on the freshness they hadn't seen in weeks.

After a couple of hours of dabbing perspiration from my brow and sweeping my hand around my eyes and ears to shoo away the gnats, I gathered the hand clippers and trowel. That's when I heard Alice call my name. I glanced around and smiled across the hedge.

She's the neighborhood gossip who is always ready

to tell the "dirt" on someone. Either that, or she'd probe for some fresh dirt she could spread about the person with whom she was talking. Even so, she's a likeable octogenarian.

"You look extra happy today," she observed. It sounded more like a disparaging remark than a pleasant greeting. I ignored the underlying insinuation and created a lilt in my response, "I'm fine." I nearly sang the declaration. It wasn't my intent to have a battle of words with my neighbor, and I wasn't about to let her bring my mood down.

She seemed not to take thought of it and chatted, "Since Frank's death I've noticed that you've done well. Emotionally, I mean. Isn't it difficult for you?" She gave me *that* smile along with one lifted eyebrow. "I mean, you cared for him for all those years. I don't want to darken your day, but doesn't it get sort of lonely? Do you feel you have to do something in order to fill the lonely hours?" Her wide-brimmed yellow hat shaded her pale complexion. "You've been pretty busy here for over two hours." She swept her hand across the panorama of flora. "Looks nice." She pulled her chin in and added, "I don't want to pry into your business. It's just that you seem, ah, well, you seem as though Frank's passing was nothing to be disturbed about." She shook her head. "Ah, please forgive me. I didn't mean it that way. I, ah, meant that you're so happy."

Obviously, she had been keeping track of me through her kitchen window. The café curtains never part, but she's always there seeing everything that goes on in my backyard. I'm certain the front drapes have stains on them where her pointed nose pokes out to take a look at the rest of the neighborhood.

I sighed. "Yes, I'm managing quite well," I admitted. "My flowers need attention whether Frank is here or not.

Sure, I miss him." I gestured toward the delicate blooms. "My lovely babies keep me busy with their specific needs." I glanced up at her with a smile. "I'm just a natural caregiver."

She pulled in her chin. "Well, I should think you'd be very distraught."

Now it was my turn to give her *that* smile and brow lift. "Not distraught," I said. With one eyebrow raised, I stared straight into her eyes. "*Relieved* is the better word."

She was taken back and almost grunted.

I added, "You have no idea just how relieved I am. Oh, I loved Frank all the way to his death. But the stress level on me was almost unbearable."

She was obviously appalled by my candor and her mouth dropped open. It was the first time I'd seen her speechless.

I nodded and turned toward the garage. "Have a nice day."

I grabbed the other garden tools and put them away. As I busied myself in the garage, I could hear Alice muttering in the distance. She wanted to tell me the latest neighborhood gossip, but I wasn't in the mood to hear what she had to say. I figure after what I told her about my feelings, she'd be spreading it around the entire bay area that I was cold and unfeeling and that I was glad Frank was dead. Of course, that isn't true. But maybe I added a nugget to her gossip repertoire. In any case I told the truth. I *am* relieved. Sure, I miss Frank and still love him. That love will never die. However, I do have moments when loneliness overwhelms me. But I'm a survivor, and I'm going to have a wonderful life—for the years I have left. And maybe, just maybe, Bill will be part of that existence. No! That's not the word I want to use. I'm not going to simply *exist*, I'm going to *live life to the fullest*.

As I headed to the house, I guess I was on one of my victory rides. My head was high and I felt like I was stepping lightly. It was a great sensation that warmed me from the top of my head to the tips of my toes.

When I brought the phone through the back door into the kitchen, I put it back into its cradle on the counter. There was Bill's number facing me again. I sighed and picked up the yellow sticky memo.

The phone rang even as I fingered the little notepaper. I checked the caller ID. *It was him.* My heart seemed to skip several beats and then do flip flops. God was answering my prayer. That realization made my heart join the Indy 500 as it raced around in circles in my chest. My hand trembled when I picked up and softly said, "Hello."

His baritone was like velvet against my ear. "This is Bill Carrington. We met at the Hospice meeting a few nights ago. Do you remember me?"

I was glad to hear my voice so calm.

My images were vivid and I thought, *Do I remember you? Are you kidding me? Of course I remember you, and I've been aching for this call for three whole days.* I pushed the thoughts back and answered, "Ah, yes Bill. I remember." *OK. Am I Ms. Cool or what?*

He was genuinely apologetic. "I hope you don't mind me calling so soon after we met."

"No. This is fine. I don't think there's a rule that says we have to wait any particular length of time before society allows us to have contact."

He chuckled. "No, I guess not. How have you been, Lilly?"

When he said my name, it carried the soft strings of tenderness; like a violin and cello in harmony. Chamber music filled my head.

I swallowed and took a deep breath. "Fine. And you?"

"Great!" He got to the point immediately. "I was wondering if you'd have lunch with me today. I'm sorry it's on such short notice. But I figured the only way to find out is to ask. So, I'm asking."

The words melted my anxieties for a split second, and then I questioned whether this was real. Was he asking me on a *date*? It's been decades since I was on a date. I choked out my answer. "I—I'm sorry. Regrettably, I have to attend an afternoon volunteer hospice meeting. I'm committed to becoming a volunteer counselor." At the same time, I was regretting that I had signed up and wanted to say that I'd just forget that and go with him. But my integrity was at stake, and I couldn't do that. I live by the Bible and Deuteronomy 23:23 teaches me not to make a vow and then fail to keep it. I thought about it. OK, I'll admit that a lot of excuses went through my mind. But I dismissed them and determined to keep my promise.

He was undaunted. "When's the meeting?"

"One o'clock," I chirped.

"I don't mean to push, but I have to ask. How long will it take?"

To my delight he was pressing for details. I answered, "They tell me that the meetings usually last about an hour."

"When the meeting's over will you meet me at the Lobster House for soup and salad?"

Here's a man who likes soup and salad. I was impressed. I could feel myself being drawn to him. "I believe I can make it by two thirty."

"Great! We'll eat about three o'clock, so it'll be kind of a supper and lunch combination. Maybe we can call it *suplunch*."

I laughed. His adaptability delighted me, and his sense of humor brought laughter for both of us. What woman doesn't like a man who can make her laugh? I was in desperate need of plenty of laughter. The conversation was abbreviated, but filled with hope and a splash of anxiety. Even before we hung up, I was verbally agonizing over what to wear on this first date. "I haven't been to the Lobster House. Will slacks be appropriate?" I asked.

He was silent.

I pulled the phone from my ear and frowned at it. When I put it back in place I asked, "Do you have a problem with a woman in slacks?"

Finally, he chuckled. "No," he said. "I wasn't hesitant because of any misgivings about women in slacks. I'm old but not old-fashioned. I was just marveling over what it's like to have a conversation with a female able to string words into intelligible sentences and understandable thought patterns. It's been a long time since I've experienced it."

He hesitated and then added, "I also remembered that you females think so far ahead of us males. When you asked about slacks, I wasn't prepared for it and was caught off guard."

"I'm sorry. I forgot that you men can only focus on one thought at a time."

He laughed and added, "And you women are wired to switch from one subject to another with ease." He was still laughing when he muttered, "Even in the middle of the first thought."

He had me there. "Well," I asked again, "what about slacks."

"Hmm," he intoned.

I jumped in. "You do have a problem with me wearing slacks." That blunt statement came out so easily that I felt like we had conversed, become instant friends, and were at a level that need not be shy or reserved. He was so easy to talk with that I almost lost myself in my reply.

He didn't respond to my direct statement but simply said, "You had on a nice dress the other night."

I pressed him. "So, you do have a problem with women wearing slacks."

"No. Not in general."

"Then would you mind if I wore slacks for this luncheon?" I was almost into frustration. I wanted him to be candid, but he was cautious. It was good that I pressed the issue, because he finally came clean and it thrilled me.

"Well ..." He dragged it out. "In your case, I do mind."

"Oh?" His statement appeared to convey the concept that we had known each other for a long time, and he was at liberty to direct my life. Even though I had that same sense of intimacy, still I was a little defensive. "In my case?" I retorted.

"Forgive me for being so bold." He chuckled. "Allow me to explain. One of the first things I noticed was your shapely legs, and I don't want them covered up with all that material."

My face was suddenly hot and I didn't know how to respond. He had noticed more about me than I realized. I guess my hesitation was prolonged and the air was dead. He observed my "shapely legs." Oh, my. At my age that compliment was beyond my ability to digest. I was without a proper response and let the phone hang on dead air. Yes, I had been a model, but that was eons ago. I wondered if he'd taken in my figure well enough to elicit such a compliment.

"Have I offended you?" he asked. "I mean, I was only attempting to show how much I admire your loveliness. Was it out of order?"

I took a deep breath. "Well, I'm just overwhelmed that

anyone would even look at my legs at this age. I was used to it when I was young, but I'm older than dirt now."

"Lilly," he scolded, "Don't put yourself down. You're a lovely lady. Your beauty hasn't faded, only grown statelier. Age has added character to your character." His voice dropped into a whisper. "You're like the country boy said about fine wine. 'The longer you set the better you get.'"

His sense of humor invited me to want to hear more. This "date" concept drew me to wonder if anything would develop while we got to know each other. *Intrigued* seems to be the operative word in this new relationship. I was so intrigued that my toes tingled. From there up my body to my brain I could feel that spark ignite in me like never before. I was suddenly alive again. Had I known that Frank's need to be cared for had actually killed my desire for life, I wouldn't have been so caught off guard by this unexpected thrill. My wondering mind considered what might be in store in these golden years. They had been so tarnished that I never even considered that anything could remove the corrosion. But here was Bill, easily polishing our relationship so that the shine of gold flickered in my heart.

Our First Date

I didn't wear slacks when I met Bill outside the restaurant; rather, a fitted dress, pale yellow with orange buttons and a colorful complementary sash around my waist. Since I'm tall and thin, I can get away with a lot of color in my outfits. It seemed to hit the spot with him, because he openly scanned my aging curves. I was almost embarrassed with the length of time he spent just staring at me. Even so, it was a delicious moment, and I drew it in and savored it. I had always wanted to have a family, but now that I was older something in me was glad that I didn't get stretched out of shape with pregnancy. Except for the sagging skin when I hold my arms out, I'm as trim and as shapely as ... well ... I'd better not go there. I want this diary to have only the truth in it. That idea really is laughable when I attempt to critique myself. It's impossible to evaluate what I've become. Oh, I can go back and look at who and what I was some years ago, but to see myself with even a modicum of understanding is not in the realm of possibility. And I don't think I'm any different from most people. If I were asked to stand in front of a crowd and evaluate myself, I'd be at a loss for words. I don't really know myself. Maybe that's why I'm sometimes aghast at what I'm writing in this journal.

That's enough ruminating. I need to get back to that

wonderful moment when Bill evaluated me and I pondered my assessment of him.

He was dapper in light-cream slacks and a deep-raspberry dress shirt that was wide open at the neck. And he wore a sport coat that many other men would have had a problem wearing. It was actually soft pink, and it fit him perfectly. The coat was a wonderful contrast to his dark tan. When I commented, "A real man," he looked askance. I touched the sport coat at his chest, rubbing the lapel. I didn't feel that my touch was too intimate for our first date, but still had reservations about it. I lifted my eyebrows. "Pink," I ventured. "Real men wear pink."

Bill chuckled. "I didn't know if it would be appropriate." He waved a hand. "Maybe it's a bit overdone." He scanned my outfit again. "But with yellow and orange on you and raspberry and pink on me, we make a flashy couple." His smile glowed. "Everyone will notice us. Maybe we need to work up a song and dance routine before we go in." His eyes crinkled at the corners and he let out an open-mouthed laugh that shook him to the core. We were still laughing as we entered the restaurant.

The smell of freshly baked bread permeated the place. "Ooh, I love that aroma," I commented.

"That's one of the reasons I've made this place a permanent part of my eatery list."

The hostess approached. "Mr. Carrington," she acknowledged.

He nodded and held up two fingers. As we followed her, he added, "The yeast rolls are out of this world." Then we were seated, and the hostess left.

"May I order drinks for us?" he asked.

"I don't really drink anything harder than wine." I wrinkled my nose. "And it's a bit early for that."

"Oh no," he assured me, "soft stuff."

I smiled and nodded.

Our waitress approached. She too greeted him by name and glanced at me.

It made me wonder if I might be just another filly in his stable. I shook the thought when he acknowledged her. "Emily. It's good to see you." He glanced at me then back to Emily. "My new acquaintance, Lilly, has allowed me to order for both of us."

She smiled and her brow lifted in anticipation.

"Two peach pamparas," he said.

Her smile broadened. "Yes, sir." She wrote down the order and left.

I tilted my head and lifted an eyebrow. "And what is a peach pampara?"

"Actually, pampara is a distorted variation of a word for glacier, or iceberg. It's a very refreshing, peach-based icy-cold drink. Maybe it'd be better if I used the term peach-ade."

The smile I put on and my raised eyebrows must have given me away.

He observed, "You look skeptical."

"Please, just tell me what I'm going to be drinking."

He glanced to one side and then leaned his elbows on the table and got close to me as though he might be revealing a deep, dark secret. He whispered, "It's peach tea over crushed ice with a cinnamon stick garnish." He put his palms up. "That's all."

I frowned. "Peach iced tea," I acknowledged. "That's it?"

"That's it," he assured.

I thought about it. "It does sound refreshing." I considered the cinnamon stick. "Cinnamon," I mused. "That's going to be very different."

The waitress arrived with two short-stemmed frosted glasses filled to the brim with the slushy amber drinks that looked to me like something from the bar. I hoped Bill was telling the truth about there not being any alcohol in these beautiful concoctions. I hate hard liquor.

He nodded toward the glasses and lifted his. "To our time together," he said. "Let's hope that this is the beginning of something special."

I lifted my glass to clink against his and echoed, "Special."

His smile broadened as he took the glass to his lips. I tentatively tasted. Swallowed and licked my lips. This peach pampara was fabulous. It was indeed refreshing and icy cold. The peach taste was not just a hint, neither was it overwhelming. It was just right. "Mmm," I moaned. When I put it down, I stirred it with the cinnamon stick to see if I could enhance the flavor just a bit with that cinnamon taste.

"You like it," he stated, as though it was a foregone conclusion.

"I do." I tasted it again and the slight bit of cinnamon was there. When I put it back on the tablecloth, I allowed my tongue to circle my lips, and I winked at him. "If this sets the tone for the rest of our afternoon, we're going to have a fantastic time."

He was obviously pleased with my assessment and asked, "Special?"

I nodded my approval of that word, but I also wondered if it would hold up for the long haul. When it comes to relationships, guys are into the immediate gratification of a hundred-yard dash, while we women are always looking at the cross-country marathon. Having a special time at a luncheon is nice, but allowing life to be special for the duration is much more fulfilling.

As our luncheon date evolved, we talked openly about

our late spouses. Bill's wife was a victim of Alzheimer's, as my Frank had been.

He said, "The dark void of a meaningful conversation that has the normal give and take is worse than death. I don't mean to sound harsh or cruel, but now that Mary's gone, I feel free to pursue relationships that were impossible in her condition. I'm not just speaking about women either. People in general are now open to me."

His eyes moistened. That impressed me. Here was a tender-hearted man who loved soups and salads, intimate conversation with people in general, and he appeared to be sensitive. What planet did he come from? I mean, they just don't make men like him anymore. Most of the men I've met are self-centered, boastful, and need to have their egos stroked at every turn—high-maintenance guys. Bill is not like that at all. He's always searching for ways to please other people. Even the smallest things don't slip by his attention. Like when I first arrived at the restaurant. He was leaning against his car. I parked next to him and he hurried around to open the car door for me. His hand steadied me as he helped me out of the car and up the steps to the entrance. Inside the restaurant he pulled out my chair and eased it under me as I sat. He even told the server that I had given him *permission* to order for me. William Harper Carrington is a gem. If this isn't God's hand in my life then I don't know what God's hand is like.

As we ate, he continued and I listened. "No one knew how much I protected my wife. Well, maybe that isn't the truth. Yes, I was protecting *Mary* all right, but more than that I was protecting myself. I couldn't bear having another couple over for dinner. I was afraid Mary would say something embarrassing for everyone. The result was that I sat alone with her. I got so tired of watching old TV reruns that I wanted to throw a brick through the screen.

I even felt like I had adopted Archie Bunker's warped sense of patriotism, racism, and twisted political beliefs." He took a deep breath and allowed his eyes to scan the restaurant. "Even this place was out of bounds near the end. In the earlier stages we came here often. But as Mary slid down that horrible Alzheimer's slide toward death, she became incorrigible. Nothing pleased her, and I couldn't talk sense to her." Bill looked into my eyes. "But you must have had the same lack of communication with your husband, so you understand." A tiny teardrop seeped out of the corner of his left eye, and he took his napkin and brushed at it and swallowed hard. His voice broke, and he repeated, "You understand."

I felt the urge to get up and step around the table to hug him—at least to pull his head against my shoulder and allow him to cry if that's what he felt he needed to do. I didn't feel right holding him, so I placed my fork in my salad bowl and reached out to enfold his hand in mine. My lips felt dry and I ran my tongue over them before I said, "Bill, the many years I had with Frank before his illness were wonderful. I know you and Mary had a great life too. It wasn't perfect even before Alzheimer's disease, but for the most part it was very, very nice. But I'll have to admit, this last decade has been ... well, agony to say the least. I didn't lose Frank when he quit breathing. I lost my husband to this dreaded disease many years before that. It didn't mean I stopped loving him. My love for Frank was as secure as ever. Sure, he was still here in body. But the man I lived with the first part of my life was gone, and this shell of a man replaced him. I know what you went through with Mary. The loneliness, the failure to have a decent conversation, and the lack of intimacy has left us with mixed emotions. I loved Frank, and I'm sorry life

turned out this way for him. Yet now that he's gone, I'm ...
I'm ..." I didn't want to admit it again.

Bill squeezed my hand. "Relieved?" he questioned.

I swallowed hard and tears attempted to surface.
"Y–yes," I choked and dabbed at my eyes. "Although I
used that very word to a neighbor, I couldn't say it to you
right now. But you saw through my hesitation. You knew
the proper word." My relief was obvious as I sighed and
slumped a little. I muttered, "You and I have been through
the very same situations. We completely understand each
other." I swallowed hard, and under my breath I uttered,
"*Thank you Lord.*"

Bill squeezed my hand a second time. "Lilly, you're
right. I've felt that same relief. But I was ashamed of my
feelings until this very moment. It's so gratifying to know
that I'm not alone. You understand just how I feel. You've
had those same thoughts and fought the same battles with
your emotions. You've experienced the prison of caring for
an Alzheimer's patient that seems to grow more binding
every day. And you're right. Our love for our spouses didn't
diminish. We still love who they were, and that won't ever
go away." He wagged his head. "Even so, the frustration of a
twenty-four/seven existence with such irrational thinking
and behavior was almost beyond a tolerable level. I came
so close to blowing my brains out." His brow rose. "I mean
it. There were times when, if I would have had a gun in the
house, I may have shot her and then shot myself. I wanted
to put her out of her misery and then take my own life."

I stared directly into his moist eyes. "But we're free,"
I whispered. "We're not shackled any longer. We can
enjoy life once again." I shook my head. "Am I being too
irreverent? Is this how I should feel? Should I express my
deepest thoughts like this?" I sensed closeness to Bill,
closeness like I hadn't experienced in over a decade.

He frowned. "Why not?" His head wobbled a little. "Why can't we be free enough and strong enough and practical enough to simply tell the world how liberating death can be for the living?" A slight smile invaded the serious expression on his face. He added, "Both Mary and Frank would want it that way."

I had to agree. This is so odd. My mind conjured up the concept that Bill and I were in a bubble of reality, and the entire world was living in fantasyland. Everyone else wanted us to grieve and carry the onus of guilt. If for a moment we might feel relief, someone was always there to push us back into the depths of despair. But that wasn't the case for us now. We had each other. We tasted freedom and joy for the first time in years. I had to agree with Bill. There was no denying that we were sad and happy all at the same time. A verse of scripture came to mind. I tried to recall where it was. In Philippians, I was certain. The apostle Paul tells us to *forget what is behind and press toward the mark of the high calling of God in Christ Jesus.* I didn't know how Bill would react to me quoting the Bible directly, so I said, "We just need to forget those things that are behind and push toward those things that are ahead."

He nodded. "That's exactly right." He pulled his hand back and started dabbling with his salad as he talked. "I'm a very practical man. I always have been. My father was practical, and his father was practical, and I've inherited that DNA. So, I'm taking a long look at life right now. I'm not into euthanizing anyone, but I can't help saying that Mary's death was liberating." He continued to dabble around in the bowl but didn't take a bite of the salad and put his fork down to look at me. "Before I went to the meeting the other night, I told both my daughter and my son that I probably wasn't going to make it another six months. I knew that my life had been wrapped around caring for Mary and that now I had no reason to live. It was as odd a mixture of feelings as I have ever encountered. I was free on one hand and yet felt a void in my life on the other. That's the best way to describe it. I felt a huge void in my existence." He glanced off to the side for a long moment. When he brought his gaze back, he was very serious. "I went to that meeting to find some sort of reason to carry on. I thought I might be able to help other people who were struggling to make sense out of all of life. I pumped myself up before opening that door so that I could at least bring the façade of happiness to anyone I came across." Bill scoffed at his own thought and added, "I'm the last guy who'd be right to counsel anyone on life and its sensibility." He took a deep breath. "But at that meeting, when I sat next to you I felt purpose come back into my life. You gave me a reason to live." His chin quivered. "It's so unusual because we didn't even talk to each other for the entire meeting. But I sensed that there was something in the air. I don't believe in karma or nirvana or godly direction or angelic pushes, but I truly felt you were the reason I was there. You gave me something to live for. Energy radiated from you." He smiled boyishly. "I'm going to admit something I promised myself I'd keep secret." He hesitated. "Believe me. When I got home and put that little piece of paper with your phone number on the dresser it was all I could do to keep myself from calling you right at that moment. I struggled with it until I finally went to sleep around two o'clock in the morning. The next day was another one of those fights with myself over that number. I memorized it and went to the phone several times. In my heart of hearts, I wanted to believe that you were waiting for my call. Then I always rationalized that I was simply nourishing my desire to have a relationship with you. That's when I finally forced myself to forget you for a day—a full day, mind you. I went out and shot a round of golf with my buddy. Steve and I got involved in that so much that I found relief from my images of you. But last night was unbearable. I tossed and turned and envisioned you in every way. That's why I called you this morning."

I felt my brow wrinkle. The combination of his announcements startled me. First, here I was thinking that *he* was the one who brought life into that room. Yet he felt that I was the one exuding a bubbling, happy life. This was getting to be spooky. Second, he had been as reticent to make the call as I was. Who is this man?

God, are You listening? What's happening here?

My silent prayers were like an SOS to the harbor master.

My ship is in trouble and I need You to rescue me.

I imagined the apostle Peter sinking into the water after he had traversed the wind and waves toward Jesus. *Help!*

Like Peter, I was grasping for the Master's hand. That concept segued into the time when Jesus was asleep in the back of the ship during a dangerous storm. Just as the disciples did, I felt I had to awaken Jesus to tell Him about this emotional hurricane trying to blow me away.

I could see that Bill's emotions were barely below the surface as well. He looked like he was about to cry. It moved me and I said, "I too saw no future. But now ... well, now I want to live and dream and run like a schoolgirl." I reached out and touched his hands again. "Bill, you may not believe this, but I went there as a last resort. The second time I went I put my name on a list when a very persuasive woman brought a clipboard around for those who may want to be volunteers. I signed up." I added a quirky expression. "As I look back on it, I believe I did that so I could wallow in self-pity." I choked back tears.

"Then, that third meeting I attended you walked through the door and all I could see was radiance. You brought light into that dismal room." I grinned. "Now you tell me you pumped yourself up so you could at least bring an artificial smile to your face in order to bring me that radiance. This is all so amazing."

His jaw dropped. He was as astonished as I was. "I don't have many more years left," he reasoned. "But now I see that what I do have can be bright and full of life. Since I met you, I made a vow to myself. I vowed to discover a new beginning. I promised myself that I would put all possible effort into taking the months and maybe years ahead and creating as much enjoyment as I am able." He tilted his head to the side and his eyebrows rose. "Is that too irrational?"

"No!" I blurted. "A new beginning is exactly what I see in this opportunity."

His brow pulled together and he sat up straight. "Then I haven't gone off the deep end?"

"If you have, hold your nose and swim your way upstream." I squeezed his hands. "I'm swimming with you. We'll jump into the deep end where the water is raging. As soon as we're over our heads we'll swim our way to shore. There'll be a luau with a pig roasting and brown-skinned men playing ukuleles. Women in grass skirts swaying their hips to the music of a Hawaiian steel guitar while their hands tell a story." I held up my glass. "And there are peach pamparas with bright red cherries on top and little umbrellas in them. People are laughing and singing. It's a new life."

"Wow!" he exclaimed. "You've got a vision. You've really got an imagination!"

"Bill, this is what we've both been waiting for all these years. Oh, I'm not saying we were just sitting around waiting for our spouses to die. What I'm saying is that we yearned for life; life the way it was intended to be lived." I patted his hands. "I'm with you. Let's discover just what God has in store for us."

Now look what I've done. This is proof that Bill Carrington has me in a tailspin, and I don't know which end is up. Before I met him at the Lobster House, I attended my potential volunteers' meeting, and it was a significant event. But here I am writing all about Bill and our luncheon date and neglecting what important things went on at the meeting.

First, the meeting was a preliminary counselor's training session. It appears I'm not as excited about being a counselor as I thought I'd be. Even so, the experience at the meeting was vital. The senior trainer, Sandra, is a very perceptive woman in her fifties whose mother was afflicted with Alzheimer's. She's been a counselor for over ten years. After introducing herself with a rundown of her qualifications, for openers she asked if we had any questions. Several of the trainees brought up some valid points, and she answered each to their satisfaction. I was reluctant, but wanted so much to ask my question that I think she saw it in my eyes and nodded toward me. So, I asked if there were any patterns in the afterlife of a caregiver once the patient had expired. Sandra gave us half a dozen typical reactions to the death of the patient but didn't cover my situation. I thanked her and put the question in a way that wouldn't reveal that I was the person needing help.

My question was something like: *Is there a typical response to the sudden lack of someone to care for that may leave the caregiver vulnerable? Making that person search out a relationship by what is becoming popular these days, dating sites, and maybe even fall in love again?*

She gave me one of those knowing smiles and then turned to the rest of the trainees and offered her answer. I thought that was so gracious of her. She took the spotlight off me and yet gave me what I needed to hear.

Sandra's answer was, "More women than men are vulnerable to the immediacy of the need to fill the void left by the deceased patient. Therefore, many women become vulnerable to those they find at online dating sites who are there to take advantage of a person's sorrow." She softened her response by saying, "But more than ever, many caregivers reach out for companionship within the community of single caregivers such as this group. And a few actually find life-mates and are genuinely happy with their new love. I believe it's more out of a common valley they've both experienced that makes them so compatible."

Of course, it's easy to see that I came away from the training session focused on my new love. So, writing about our luncheon and forgetting my question and answer was normal. I have to laugh. Just using that word *normal* doesn't feel normal. Lately I'm wondering just what normal is.

Even thinking that way has made me consider my newfound relationship with Bill. Is either of us functioning properly? Have we been with our abnormal circumstances long enough to warp our thinking? Is Bill all that he seems to be? Or, is he reacting out of desperation, much like I might be? That brings me to a new crescendo in my assessment of this love dream. Now, I'm wondering what will happen if we continue seeing each other and then the ultimate happens. Are we sane enough to handle a long-term relationship? OK, I'll write my heart here. What if we get all the way to the altar? Will we be certain that we are capable of handling a normal marriage?

Again, I'm thinking so far ahead of the curve that I know I'm not rational. I'm simply a dreamer who needs to get her feet on the ground.

Help, Lord!

Our First Picnic

oward the end of the week, Bill called and asked if I wanted to go to Taylor Park for a picnic on the lush green grass near the lake. It was as if I had become a schoolgirl again, and I giggled inside as I thought about it. My answer was no answer at all. I said, "I haven't been on a picnic since I was a child." I spoke my thoughts. "My memories of a picnic are a woven wood-slatted basket with double lids that hinged in the middle. That's how long it's been."

Bill chuckled. "Yes," he said, "That was the highlight of our family picnics too."

I said, "That basket sat on my mother's checkered table cloth spread on the grass." The vivid childhood scene inched across my mind, and I savored every image.

Even though I was eager to go with Bill, I tried to sound casual. "That would be nice to relive those memories I suppose," I intoned. Inside, I was jumping up and down. I didn't question my feelings, because I was afraid I'd become rational and ruin this euphoric trance. My heart was young again, and there was no reason to question my feelings.

"Is that an affirmative?" He sounded a bit dejected.

"I think so." I was playing the hook like a professional fisherman.

He added, "If you're questioning what to bring, don't worry about it. You won't have to bring a thing. I'll fix it all. I'm well equipped to handle it from the opening of cans to unscrewing jar lids. I can even open a bag of chips." I laughed. "Super strong if you can do that." He chuckled. "Honestly, please don't bring anything. I'll have it all taken care of."

I was taken aback. "Nothing?" I questioned.

"Just bring your wonderful radiance." He laughed. "That'll put the sun to shame."

We added a little small talk. I attempted to continue to be casual, but the more he spoke of our time at lakeside the more the little girl in me wanted to burst.

We said our goodbyes, and the phone was silent.

I replaced the handset in its cradle and leaned against the counter wondering if Bill Carrington was really as romantic as all that. Was he putting on just to woo me into ... Uh, oh! I didn't want to think about that. I muttered to myself, "Relax, Lilly. Take it in stride."

I checked the weather report. It was going to be an extra warm day so I slipped into navy-blue shorts and a crisp, white blouse. My sandals had two-inch heels, and that gave a little extra curve to my calves. Yes, I'll admit I had Bill's attraction to my legs in mind, and wanted to entice him. I wore a straw hat with a muted navy and powder-blue band and carried a straw purse. All that made me feel outdoorsy and in the mood for a full-blown picnic. Again my childhood memories kicked in, and I saw Uncle Vern pitching horseshoes while we girls played badminton across a tight net. Creating wonderful memories is what the first half of life is about—that way we can relive them several times during the second half of our existence.

When I drove to Bill's home, he answered the door immediately, and when I saw him, I was *wowed*. He looked so handsome in his floral Hawaiian shirt, loose at the waist, and navy-blue Bermuda shorts. He too wore a straw hat with the trim above the brim made of the same material as his shirt. It appeared we agreed on our outfits before we saw each other. That, of course, wasn't the case. It just happened that we both had navy blue on our minds. It was amazing. Cream deck shoes finished his outfit. He was classy all the way and far from the longshoreman I'd first imagined.

I pointed at him. "You did it!"

"So did you," he uttered. "Navy blue is the color of the day."

I shook my head. "Not that as much as ..." I scanned him from head to toe.

He pulled back. "I did what then?"

"You bought this outfit because I told you that we would swim to the shore where a luau was in progress." I spread my hands toward him. "You really caught the same vision I described." I pointed at his hat. "You're trying to make my imagination come to life." I put my fists on my hips. "And ... navy blue," I added.

His mouth twisted into a sideways grin. "I guess I'm just a little boy at heart. I wanted to please you, and ... well, I figured this would do it. For me, the navy blue is my way of enhancing the nautical idea. After all, we'll be at the lake. So, this is the way I see it." He turned as though he might be modeling it.

Without thinking, I lunged forward, threw my arms around his neck and kissed him on the cheek. When I stepped back, I said, "I'm extremely pleased."

He scanned my outfit. "I like it," he chirped. Then his voice softened, and the deep baritone added, "Beautiful legs."

Although I felt a little uneasy, I simply said, "Thank you."

"What do we do from here?" he asked. He stepped forward and put his arms around my waist.

I pulled my chin in, lifted an eyebrow and said, "A picnic in the house isn't my idea of a picnic at all." I pushed him back and smirked. "Maybe we'd better go to the park and have our picnic there."

He snapped his fingers as though I'd given him a sudden revelation. "That's a great idea!" We left his place for the full day.

We drove down Eighth Avenue to the entrance to Taylor Park. When we got to the lake, Bill pulled a large cardboard box out of the trunk and placed it on the grass. He withdrew a blanket and I helped him spread it on the ground. He didn't allow me to bring anything to this outing, and I felt uncomfortable. But when the display was unveiled from a large cooler, I was again taken by surprise. Bill hadn't forgotten one thing. Everything a picnic should have was spread on the blanket. He even provided linen napkins. He is so unlike any man I've ever met.

We had a delightful time sitting on the blanket and lightly chatting as we prepared paper plates of potato chips, baked beans and grilled chicken wings; along with all the relish trimmings. He brought a drink I wasn't sure of, but he said I'd like it. "It's made of freshly frozen fruit and mango-peach punch with a splash of cranberry juice cocktail. I put it in the blender with crushed ice so that it becomes a smoothie with wonderful flavor." He shook the thermal jug and then poured the frozen delight into a red plastic cup. When it was filled with the concoction he added, "And it's good for you."

I tried the slushy mixture. It was cold and refreshing with a hint of tang accenting the sweetness. Actually, the balance was just right to modify the salty potato chips.

While we were eating, Bill kidded me about an alligator in the water that may come up and grab me. He said, "And I'll wrestle him back into the lake. I'd hate to see him put even a tiny scratch on such beautiful legs. They look like the Florida sun has kissed them into a golden hue."

I acted embarrassed, but was delighted. He had emphasized the perfection of my legs enough for me to realize that Bill was indeed *a leg man*. That's when our relationship began to mess with my mind. We had known each other for less than a week and here I was feeling physical stimulation. My body was responding to his verbal observations. Something was stirring in me that I had assumed was dead and buried. When he looked at my legs and made his comment, I could feel the tingling sensation I had felt as a virgin when Frank and I came together on our honeymoon. My thoughts were fighting with each other. *Should I feel this way? I'm a senior citizen for goodness sakes. But I'm still human.* The phrases in my mind tumbled over each other like a bunch of puppies at play. I lay back on the blanket and stared up at the green leaves of the water oak shading our spot on the lake's bank. Beyond the leaves the blue sky was like a canopy of security. The sun was warm, and I felt like God was smiling down on us. The breeze that had been there earlier was gone, and the rush of warm sun splashing through the leaves felt relaxing. His hand touched my shoulder and I turned to look up into his serene gaze.

He whispered, "Lilly." His smile was brighter than the sunlight. "This is the picture your name brings to mind." He put his hand on mine and continued to stare into my eyes. "Lilly," he whispered again. "You're the picture of the freshness of springtime. You're the sweet fragrance of new petals in the early morning. You are the kiss of sunshine warming my entire being."

He was so poetic. I ate it up. At that moment I felt like I was a teenager again. I couldn't see my wrinkles, so my self-image was of youthful vigor. That gave me a devil-may-care attitude. Joy filled my heart, and I returned to my younger days. Bill was still flowing with poetic phrases, and I closed my eyes and listened. If this wasn't heaven, it was as close as a person could get to it and still be here on earth.

The warm air, the bright sunshine, and the blue sky with its puffy white clouds and the occasional gentle breezes made this lakeside picnic as perfect as perfect could be. I imagined that nothing could spoil these moments we were having together.

Then, a snapshot of Frank crossed my mind. I wondered if I was forgetting my dead husband. *Was this happening too fast? Should I have refused this date?* I guess my mood was shattered and I wasn't hiding it very well, because Bill asked what was wrong.

I opened my eyes. "What could be wrong?" I retorted.

His gaze flitted about as though he might be searching for the answer. "I don't know. Your brow wrinkled and you just seemed to be distant all the sudden." He was serious. "Did I say something that offended you?"

I sat up and put my hand on his jaw. The feel of stubble in my palm was reassuring. Bill was all man. I softly stated, "Nothing's wrong. It's just that I'm unsure of our timing. I mean, Mary and Frank are hardly gone and here we are enjoying life as though ..."

He put his finger on my lips. "Lilly. Please listen to me. The fact is they *are gone*. No one can deny that. Whether we wait a day, a week, five months, or three years, some people will never think it's long enough. There'll always be those who believe we should live in sorrow the rest of our lives. You'll find a group who refuses to allow us the freedom to live again." He shook his head. "I'm not going to listen to them. I'm going to live and love and enjoy life. I hope you're with me on this. We deserve a second chance. A fresh start. We put in our time of devotion and, ah, duty, so to speak. We followed our vows, and now we're free to live again."

I had to nod and agree with him.

He added, "Time will never bring Frank or Mary back. One day we'll be gone too. People will grieve for a moment or two and then go on with their lives just like we need to do."

It was foolish of me to dismiss the opportunity God presented for me with Bill. I had to think rationally and realize that this was my chance at life. Or, I could just lie down and die before my time. It was up to me. The option reminded me of a Bible study I was in some months back. The teacher was focused on Deuteronomy 30:19. In essence, God is saying to Israel, "I set before you life and death; choose life, so that you and your household may live and prosper." Right there, at that very moment I decided to choose life. My mind captured that verse from Philippians again. *Forgetting what is behind* ... Hmm. It's so easy to say and so difficult to do.

Another thing hit me. After more than ten years as a New York model, I was known as a tough cookie. That temperament has been my aura. Everyone knew not to mess with me, because I have always been a determined woman. But that was before I met Jesus. That was when I was my own boss. I'm not that egotistical, highly practical woman any more. Well, maybe I'm still somewhat practical. However, I don't make a big deal about being practical like I used to. Instead, I pray about everything and look to the Lord for direction. Even so, I find myself wrestling with my thoughts and sometimes giving in to my emotions. The *old me* rises up to take control and call on my practical processing side. Now, with Bill in my life, I'm fighting urges that have been latent for so long I don't even remember when I last felt this way. I'm attempting to be practical about Bill, but emotions rise up and I wilt. This tough cookie has gotten her practical self into an emotional pickle.

Our Next Date

Bill called me and asked me to allow him to fix lunch for us at his place. At first, I attempted to assuage my conscience by telling him it was my turn to treat him to lunch. But he was very assertive and said it would be my turn next time. After volleying with him about our commitments and the balance of giving, I finally agreed to go to his place. When I had stopped by before, I didn't even get to stay for a minute before we were off to the picnic. After the outing, I simply got in my car and drove home. Dusk was setting in and I don't like to drive after dark. This time it would be much different. I was a little edgy about being alone with him in his home, but rationalized that we were adults—and although he professed no faith in God, I was certain he was a gentleman.

When I arrived at his home, he was cooking freshly caught scallops. He kissed me lightly at the door and quickly went back to the battered scallops. "They're frying in light coconut oil," he said.

I sniffed. "The aroma is wonderful."

He was busy turning the little mollusks in the pan. "Just be a few more minutes," he said without turning to look my way.

I thought Kitty would really like the scent of fried

scallops that clung to my clothing. When I got home, I'd have to push her away. She loves seafood. That thought made me aware of the fact that Bill would have it made with my cat. She'd follow him around and love him silly. Under my breath I grunted at the thought that bounced around in my head.

He has it made with me. I follow him around and love him until I'm silly.

I checked out the dinette table. A large salad and a chilled glass of Zinfandel sat on the teakwood table. I swiped my hand across the fine wood and asked, "Where did you acquire this wonderful dinette set." I noted the chairs were made of the same wood and were well crafted.

Bill laughed as he worked and still didn't look at me. "I got the wood from a marine dealer."

There I was again, aghast at what he was telling me. "You mean you made this outfit?"

Bill glanced over his shoulder with a little-boy smile spread across his face. "Have a seat. I'll be right there to sip some wine with you." He held up his glass and turned the scallops again. "I hope you don't mind that all we're having is scallops and salad. It's not much variety, but there are plenty of fresh scallops, the lettuce is crisp and the tomatoes are vine ripe and flavorful. I didn't put onions in the salad because I wasn't sure if you liked them raw. There's ranch dressing or creamy Italian, or, I have a cruet of zesty raspberry vinaigrette if you like." He waved some tongs over his shoulder. "I went out early this morning and got this catch. The scallops are plentiful if you know where to go. I find them on the sandbar just out from the municipal pier."

My mind was spinning. I thought, *What an amazing man.* I tried to contain my awe of him. After a deep breath I said, "You're so thoughtful."

He cocked his head and lifted his brow. "Have a seat at the table."

I didn't sit. "You said you went out for the scallops this morning so they can't be any fresher. How do you get them?"

He turned to grin at me. "I take my boat out to the sandbar about two hundred yards off the shore near the Clearwater pier and put on my mask and snorkel. I use a small hand rake and mesh net and pick up as many as I think I'll need. They congregate around the reedy vegetation on the bar. Within an hour or so I can gather what I think I'll use and then I'm heading back in to clean 'em up and fry 'em golden brown. That's why you see me turn them so often. I want them just right for you."

I could feel my gaping expression. "You mean you went out this morning just to feed me fresh scallops?"

This time he didn't look over his shoulder at me but added, "Just for you, sweet lady."

"Isn't it dangerous being out there alone?"

He waved and said, "Have a seat at the table. It'll only be a couple more minutes with these, and when we eat I'll tell you about the danger."

I glanced into the living room. "Do you mind if I go around and just take in the beauty of your home?"

"Not at all." He frowned at me and then added a grin. "So, you want to check me out to see what kind of housekeeper I am. I understand. Don't worry. As you can see, it's a small home. Not much to do. When Mary quit housekeeping about twenty years ago, I picked it up. I've been doing it ever since." He smiled at me. "And, because you were coming over, I made certain to lift every lamp and every picture when I dusted. And I even did the windows so you could see into the yard." He chuckled and turned back to the scallops.

I smiled at his back and eased toward the spacious living room. Sheers caressed the front tinted windows. I thought, *That's a Floridian for you. He wants things light and airy, yet his practical side tells him to block out the sun's harmful rays.* A few pictures on the walls and some statuary on the coffee table spoke volumes to me. One picture was of him and Mary on a beautiful sailboat. I called toward the kitchen, "Do you sail?"

"I did," he said.

"I see a picture of you, and I assume it's Mary on the deck of this large sailboat. Do you still have it?"

"No. I sold it to my buddy, Walter Peppers. The good thing about that deal is that Walt wants me to do the upkeep on her so he allows me to take her out any time I want to."

I made my way back into the kitchen. "You're a sailor? And what else have you done that would intrigue an old city girl?"

He finished turning the scallops for the last time and ambled over to the table and lifted his glass. "To us," he said.

I raised my glass to touch his. "To us," I repeated.

When his glass left his lips, he licked them and then answered my question. "Well, when I was young, I was one of three partners in a machine shop in Detroit just after the Big War, and did fairly well. Our shop made the punches that were used to punch holes in the sheet metal that carmakers molded to make car doors, hoods, and trunks. We hit it right at the growing point of the industrial revolution. It was lucrative. That allowed me to try several things. I did some bow hunting for deer. Duck hunted. Went into the fields to hunt pheasant and raised a couple of Pointers and an English Setter to help me hunt. After that I turned to breeding and training dogs. Boxers were the breed I chose, and I entered them into dog shows. I had a couple win a few blue ribbons and two silver cups. That was just a phase I went through. During all that I fly fished for rainbow trout in the Au Sable River."

He brought the platter of scallops over as he talked. "Once I caught a four-pound brown trout in Shoe Pack Lake up near Lovells, Michigan. I had my own iceboat and sailed around the frozen spots near Detroit. Then I met a guy, Fred Bauer, and he taught me how to fly single-engine planes. I got my pilot's license and bought an Aircoupe. I sold it and then bought and sold a few other planes." He motioned to me as though to say he was through speaking for the moment, and we needed to get on with the eating.

We sat down and I asked if he minded if I said grace. He shrugged and bowed his head. When I finished, he added, "Amen."

Bill dished up the scallops and salad and continued telling me about his life. It was so interesting that I kept prodding him for more.

He obliged, "Then, when I moved the family down here to the Largo-Clearwater area, I bought a trailer court. My son, Tim, and I turned it into a mobile-home park for retirees. That was a lot of work."

I bit into the first scallop and moaned. "Oh, this is delicious."

Bill smiled and asked, "You don't mind if I continue while we eat, do you?"

"Oh, no, of course not. It's intriguing."

"I want you to tell me more about your life, but I thought you needed to know who you're sitting with so it'll give you a better understanding of just what you might encounter. I'm a bit overzealous for life. I want to cram as much living into my years as possible. If you continue seeing me, I want you to know what you may encounter."

I tasted the salad and nodded. "That's wonderful."

Bill went on. "I built radio-controlled model airplanes right here in this house. It wasn't long before I discovered radio-controlled sailboats and built one from scratch in the back bedroom and sailed it on Freedom Lake." He hesitated.

I nodded. "What else?" I asked.

"Hmm. Intriguing things, you said." He shrugged. "I guess that's about all the intriguing things I've done." He chuckled. "I'm sure you don't want to hear about some of the other things. Some of which I'm not very proud and others are just plain dull." He smirked. "Guess I've already given you more information than you wanted anyway."

I was overwhelmed. "My goodness. No! From just what you told me I can see you've had a full and interesting life."

"I think it's been fun," he said. After a forkful of salad, he dabbed the napkin at his mouth and added, "I have a bucket list that includes parasailing, skydiving, whitewater rafting, zip line, and spelunking."

My eyes widened, and I could feel my brow lift. "Are you serious?"

His smile gleamed. "Well, at my age, the bucket is full, and I'm going to have to forego a few of those things." After spearing another scallop, he sighed. "I just wish I had another life to live."

I put my fork down. "You were going to tell me about the danger involved in going out to the sandbar for scallops. Yet everything in your bucket list smacks of danger. You don't have a death wish, do you?"

He chuckled. "No, just a taste for the intriguing things of life that carry a smidgen of risk." His left eyebrow lifted as he winked at me. "That's why I want to be with you."

"Am I a risk? Something as dangerous as scalloping?" He smiled and twisted his mouth. "Scalloping is not dangerous if you keep track of what's going on around you and make proper preparations." He ate some of the salad, and then went on. "I was in serious danger only once," he intoned.

I noticed that he had sidestepped the concept of me being dangerous. Maybe I'd prod him a little later to see if he considered me a risk of some sort. I listened as he continued.

"Mary was able to stay alone back then, so I decided to do exactly what I did this morning. But what I didn't do at that time was secure everything from the start. And it wasn't a morning outing, rather late afternoon. I was at my favorite place, a couple hundred yards from Clearwater pier. I put on my mask and snorkel and with rake in hand I eased myself over the side of the boat down onto the sandbar and found plenty of scallops. I got so involved with raking and then reaching down to pick them up and put them in the bag that I didn't notice the tide was coming in pretty fast." He shook his head. "That's one thing I forgot to do, check the tide chart. That was my big mistake. The other was being out there alone in the evening. The tide came in to the point of lifting the bow of the boat and dragging the anchor off the sandbar. Before I realized it the boat was adrift in the open Gulf waters and I was stuck on the sandbar. I could still see the boat, but she was too far away for me to swim to her."

I could feel my wrinkled brow distorting my forehead. I was alarmed by his story. "What did you do? I mean, how did you get off the sandbar?"

"First, you have to know that the sandbar is only a couple hundred yards from shore. I was within sight of the late evening beachcombers, but no one knew I was stuck out there. As the tide came in and the sun went down I got to the point where I had to tread water."

"Why didn't you swim in to shore?"

He hung his head and gave me that little-boy grin. "I had a nice mess of scallops and didn't want to leave them and my rake behind. The bag was too heavy to allow me to swim with it."

I grimaced.

"I know that it sounds really foolish now." He put another scallop in his mouth and pushed it to the side. "But these babies are delicious and hard to come by if you don't know where to go." He chewed and swallowed before he said, "Anyway, I was out there a few hours and it was getting dark. When the pier lights came on, I waved and called for help to the men fishing off the pier. They waved back but couldn't hear me shouting. They must have figured I was some teenager out there with a surfboard."

I put my fork down. I couldn't continue to eat and urged him on. "Tell me how you got rescued." I chuckled. "You must have been rescued." I waved a hand toward him. "You're here."

"Yes, I'm here and I did get rescued." He took another bite and continued. "Well, that day my good friend and fishing buddy, Doctor Webber, went by the house and asked Mary where I was. She said she didn't know. That was typical. Because of her fading ability to combine thoughts and deliver a logical response, I got in the habit of writing down my intent on a pad near the phone. I always did that, and Doc knew it. He was fully aware of Mary's condition and asked her if he could use the phone to call around to find me. Of course, he spotted the note and called the Coast Guard."

"So, they came and got you."

"Well, it wasn't that easy. I was out there in the

dark waters and I could see the Coast Guard cruiser's searchlight skimming the surface of the murky water, but they couldn't see me. I waved and shouted and nearly lost my voice entirely. It took about forty-five minutes for them to find me. By then my arms and legs were tired of treading water and I was actually taking a deep breath and then blowing it out. That allowed me to sink to the bottom to rest and then push myself back up to float as best I could."

I was astounded. "Oh, I would have been in a panic. What about sharks?"

He shook his head. "I was pretty close to panic mode myself. Yes, I considered I was shark bait, but there were none in the area."

"At least it was a happy ending."

He laughed. "I still had my bag of scallops for the day so it was a very happy ending."

What a great sense of humor. I echoed his laughter.

As we ate, I asked more about his past. He shared with me in a very open and honest way. He stopped at one point and wanted to hear all about my life. In turn, he was willing to tell me whatever I wanted to know about his marriage, his children and grandchildren, his life's work, and his deepest feelings. He's a very unusual man, not secretive like so many men. Bill is tender, even with his words. Sometimes I feel like this is nothing more than a dream. It couldn't be real, it's too perfect. Yet it is real and he's *almost* perfect.

One thing he said made me realize he was not a ten. Although he said *amen* after I said grace over the meal, he was reluctant to talk about God and faith. In fact, Bill admitted that he wasn't sure there was even a Being who created all this and is watching over it. That was strange since he was so kind, loving, and gentle—all characteristic of a godly person.

After questioning him about faith, he made a declaration that set the tone for our relationship. "Just because I admit I'm not sure about this God thing doesn't make me an evil man. I'm just practical and determined not to fall for some hocus-pocus, medicine-man-cure-all sales job. I want to step back and take a long look before I dive into any commitment that could alter the rest of my life."

"And beyond," I added.

He looked at me with a mixture of skepticism and wonder.

I thought of Frank Peretti and said, "I know about a man who speaks on the theory of evolution. He's a creationist and kind of puts evolution in its place when he says that they tell us that they say it goes from 'goo to you by way of the zoo.'"

At first, Bill chuckled.

I repeated, "'Goo to you by way of the zoo.' Pretty catchy, huh?"

He frowned. "Okay, I'll agree to that point. Evolutionists say we all came from slop in a pond, then evolved to tadpoles and monkeys, and finally became humans. Of course, that's a bunch of hooey too."

"So, you don't believe that theory?"

Bill laughed. "Not on your life. That's it! It is just a *theory*; an idea that has no credence." He licked his lips. "I can't go for the extension of that theory either. They try to make you believe that some little tadpole grew thin-skinned wings and flew around until he grew feathers so he could adapt better to the environment." He grimaced. "And then they tell us that some of them grew hair and became monkeys. However ..."

When he lifted a finger, I knew what was coming.

"It's difficult for me to think that all this we're experiencing with our five senses came together by chance. I mean, if rocks in the atmosphere started banging into each other until they formed planets then how did the planets become perfectly round with no large jutting rocks sticking out that would be visible from outer space? How come they're all so perfectly round? It just doesn't make sense either." He took a deep breath. "Not only that, my sweet Lilly; I've studied this idea of the survival of the fittest and natural selection. The proponents of *that* hogwash are trying to make me believe that a chimp that births a deformed or unique model of chimpanzee will bring it up so it can go out and find another uniquely different chimp that happens to be of the opposite sex and then they have babies that become another species all together. That's absurd! It's a proven fact that most deformed babies in the animal kingdom are rejected; either left on their own by their mother, or they are outcasts of the particular group. They have little to no chance of survival. Then to believe they actually do survive and go out into the world to find another deformed mate that happens to be exactly like him is unthinkable." He took a breath, sat back, and sighed. "But a Supreme Being? Where did He come from? Or is He a She?" His brow rose. "As you can see, I've pushed back, and for years I've taken a long, hard look at all the theories out there. And I just won't be forced into religion for the sake of saying I belong to such-and-such an organization or church, or cult, or anything." His voice rose at the end of his declaration, and the arteries in his neck bulged. Bill was adamant about how he viewed the supernatural. To him, it seemed, if it didn't fit into the five senses then he was going to reject it as "hogwash."

I had to agree, but added, "At our age, we're running out of the luxury of taking too much time to analyze and make a determination. That's why God asks us to have faith. His Word says that without faith it is impossible to please Him."

Bill shook his head as he pleasantly poo-pooed away my logic. I immediately came to the conclusion there's no doubt that *we have a problem*. And it looks like we won't be able to solve it overnight. He'll have to see how faith can make him free to make proper choices. I'd like to be the one to help him make that decision. Am I ready to take on such a daunting task? Hmm. I'll really have to think long and hard about that. I'm laughing as I write this because I had warned him about not having the luxury of too much time, and now I want the time to think long and hard. Oh well.

After we finished the meal, he was going to place the dishes in the dishwasher, but I thought there were so few that I suggested that we wash the dishes together. At that point our second problem surfaced. It was very innocent at first. I washed, and Bill was supposed to dry. But somehow we began a playful display of abandon and splashed dishwater on each other. That's when he slid around in back of me. Ever so gently he slipped his arms around my waist and eased my hands down into the warm soapy water and held them there. His hands were gentle as they moved over mine. The sensation was electrifying. The warm water covering our hands sent sensual waves through my body. It was as though our hands were making love right there in the kitchen, under sudsy water. I wanted to savor the romantic moment, but he was laughing and it was infectious. I turned to the side to laugh with him. I guess I must have given him *that look*, because he stopped laughing and his eyes locked on mine. The power of that testosterone/estrogen connection filled the air, and I swallowed. His face was so close to mine. Determination in his gaze bore a hole in my spirit. He drew closer, his chest against my back. I could feel the warmth of his breath as he turned me around to face him. His lips moved past my cheek and drew near my left ear. My left hand voluntarily gripped his shoulder. We just stood there for a very long moment. It was an instant that will live in my memory for as long as I breathe.

Then. The kiss.

It was light at first.

After that first touch of his lips, I knew I had to have more. Although our hands were out of the water, they were still dripping wet. My right hand covered the back of his neck. His masculine hands were around my waist. I could feel the dampness penetrating the back of my blouse. Our lips searched for connection, and then they were together. The wet warmth of our mouths gave way to deeper kisses. I knew at that moment my dream was reality. His hands were moving up my back as he was pulling me against his body. Although I desperately wanted what he was offering, I wasn't emotionally ready for such intimacy and eased him away.

"Is something wrong?" he whispered.

I took a deep breath. "This is a little more dessert than I anticipated," I joked.

That witty comment made Bill laugh out loud. The dessert concept really struck him, and he continued to laugh for several seconds. When he stopped laughing, he became very serious and held my chin in one hand and pushed a wisp of hair away from my forehead with the other. "Lilly, you are a delight. You make me laugh like I haven't laughed in years. You make me cry tears of joy because of the happiness you've brought into my life. And you make me thankful all at the same time."

Maybe I shouldn't have done it, but I took advantage of the opportunity and asked, "To whom are you thankful?" I must had donned a very serious expression that made him frown.

His brow pulled together at the bridge of his nose. "What do you mean?"

"You said you were thankful." I waved a hand. "When someone is thankful it's because of what someone else did for them. Who is that someone?"

He shook his head. "It's you, of course."

I could see that he was puzzled, so I made a stab at explaining. "Me?" I questioned. "I didn't do anything special. I certainly didn't arrange for us to meet at the grief counseling group. I didn't create the timing that led to all this. I didn't answer the call of two hearts yearning for a relationship of substance." I put my right hand on my chest. "Not me." I glanced up and then focused on his gaze.

He frowned and his shoulders sagged. "You're not going to shove religion down my throat, are you?" He was very serious. "That would ruin a good thing before it genuinely gets started." His hands dropped to his sides, and he turned away.

I followed him toward the living room. When I caught up with him, I put my arms around his neck and leaned my body against his back. With my strangle hold on him I was able to nibble on his ear lobe.

It must have given him that same electric sensation it gives me. In any case, it took care of his negative feelings, and he turned back to wrap his arms around my waist. He was still very serious and said, "I won't force anything on you." He pressed his lips together. "And please," his eyebrow lifted, "don't force anything on me."

Our Romantic Struggles

I t's been a long time since I've entered anything in this journal. Our whirlwind romance has zapped my mind, and love has smitten my heart. For days I've walked around in a pink cloud that has me reeling. I'm totally oblivious of time and space. I feel like what astronauts must feel when they float around above the earth. The euphoria is wonderful. Even the danger is there. Well, I guess that may be overstating what I sense. For me there is an element of intrigue that smacks of risk. But I have to come back to put my feet on the ground and make sense of all that's happening to me (us). All I can picture is the old '50s soda fountain at the local drugstore, Bobby socks and crinolines, pegged pants and hot rods, and two dizzy teenagers in love. That's funny, because we are far from teenagers. But I will say I'm experiencing *Happy Days* all over again. Unfortunately, those moments pass, and I face reality once again. All I have to do is check the mirror and discover that truth that brings me back to the real world.

Being ancient and yet living this dream puts me at odds with myself. I persist in looking in that bathroom mirror and wondering, *Why?* Why would I, of all people, be given this second chance at love? Then I rationalize it by talking to my image. "I paid my dues. Those long years of giving my love and care to Frank were not easy.

I could endure it only because of my deep love for him."
Those words would assuage my wonder of it all. That's
when I'd rekindle my positive approach and tell my image
the truth. "At times I wanted to scream. It was agony. But
I've put that aside, and I'm focused on this new romance."
Smiling at my reflection, raising my chin in triumph, I'd
turn and walk out of the bathroom in victory. I remember
one time muttering, "I'm worthy of having my fling."

Bill and I have known each other for nearly two months,
and our relationship has progressed swiftly. Maybe it's
moved a bit too rapidly for me at times. It's not that I don't
want us to test the waters of our friendship and see if it
can develop into something more than this cotton-candy
kid's stuff. I long for something more substantial, but I
keep thinking of Frank and Mary. People will talk if Bill
and I get too close too soon. Then again, just as we've
discussed, what do we care what people think? At our
age it doesn't matter. The general population forms an
opinion on almost everything before it comes into being
anyway. Nothing we say or do will change the majority
of those judgmental souls. Although I want to live my life
with integrity and display a right spirit toward others, I'm
foremost a Christian, and I care about what God thinks.
Of course, that takes me into watching my developing
life with Bill, and I have to admit that I'm confused. I've
been taught that *God is not the author of confusion.* I'm
wondering if I'm the one creating this turmoil. Should I
just go with the flow of our relationship? Do I really believe
that God put the two of us together? Was this meeting just
a chance encounter that we're both taking advantage of
because we have needs that we want fulfilled? Oh, here I
go again. This struggle is too much for me. I don't know.
I'm so anxious to have what seems to be forbidden by my
own standards of what and who a Christian is that I can't

think straight. Have I been taught incorrectly? Should I feel these romantic feelings at this point in my life? I'm so full of questions and so empty of answers.

Oh, God! Where are You?

A sudden thought just struck me. I recall a time when I was a freshman model and there was a seasoned veteran in the dressing room with the rest of us. She wore thick makeup to cover her deep wrinkles, added a lot of bright red lipstick and, at her age, spoke of being able to have boyfriends and romance. I guess she caught me looking at her dabbing on pancake an inch thick with a critical eye because she stared at me and said, "You look like you don't think I can attract men." She laughed. "Sweetie, you're going to be this age one day. All that uplift and taut skin is going to sag and look like alligator flesh. But that won't deter you from being what every man dreams of. You'll cover up the wrinkles and swing those aging hips because, no matter how old a gal is, romance is never dead in her. Everyone wants to have someone who cares, someone who will give her that romantic sensation." She flipped a pointed finger at me and added, "Just remember, young lady, you're never too old for romance."

The recall of her declaration made me think of what happened this past Sunday. Pastor Hassler hit me between the eyes with his sermon. At that moment I was stunned by the text he used. It was none other than Philippians 3:12–15. He read from the *New Century Version,* and it was as though he spoke my own mind. He read the words of the apostle Paul:

> I do not mean that I am already as God wants me to be. [I'll say amen to that.] I have not yet reached that goal, but I continue trying to reach it and to make it

mine. Christ wants me to do that, which is the reason he made me his ... I know that I have not yet reached that goal, but there is one thing I always do. Forgetting the past and straining toward what is ahead, I keep trying to reach the goal and get the prize for which God called me through Christ to the life above. All of us who are spiritually mature should think this way, too. And if there are things you do not agree with, God will make them clear to you.

I've pondered those verses and asked God to reveal to me exactly what He wants out of my relationship with Bill. I need Him to make everything clear to me. As I consider it, I believe my problem is that I'm starved for affection. So that older model was absolutely right when she preached to me about never growing out of the desire to be romanced. I truly need romance. Frank couldn't provide it for so many years. Now Bill is in my life to give me that passion that's so fulfilling. That's why I'm acting like a kid. Because of this starvation, my need to be loved is heightened. Such statements as I've just made show that I can think rationally at times. Then at other times I'm as spacey as Betty White's character Rose Nylund from *The Golden Girls*. That leads me to realize that Bill is, like any man, attaching sexual fulfillment to romantic fulfillment. All the more reason I need to restrain myself. But how? I'm so fulfilled when I'm with Bill that his concept of sexual consummation has impacted me. The importance of his lack of faith seems to diminish in the light of our romance and our physical attraction. Then, like now, when I'm putting this entry into my journal, when I'm away from him, I see clearly that our relationship can't go much further until he has a Jesus experience. Although I too want to consummate our relationship, I can't allow myself that luxury. How will I keep Bill at bay in that area and still keep Bill? I believe the only way is if Bill surrenders to faith in Christ.

Lord, reveal Yourself to Bill like You did to Saul of Tarsus on the dusty road to Damascus. Bill says he's a practical man, yet he isn't thinking like one. Please knock some sense into his spirit, Lord.

We call each other every day. Bill's voice is like honey on the palate of my mind. That makes me all the more anxious to be in his arms. I've even gotten to the point of smelling his scent that lingers in my nostrils. What's happened to me? I was in love with Frank, but I never acted like a child about it. But with Bill I'm ... I'm ... oh, I can't even put it into words. How does a woman explain the enchantment she feels for a man she barely knows? If I were to share my feelings with any of my friends, they'd have me committed. Even so, I'm in love, and I know that Bill loves me too.

When I awaken each morning, I sense an unusual expectancy. It's such a contrast with my years of waking to dread the day as I cared for Frank's every need. I feel like I'm casting doubt on my love for my husband. It isn't that I didn't love Frank. That isn't the case at all. I guess I keep defending myself on this point. But I did love him dearly. The problem was that I just got tired of pouring out that love and never taking in anything. I wanted my husband to hold me like he used to, but he couldn't. Oh, he could physically put his arms around me, but his mind wouldn't, or couldn't think in those terms. Even if I snuggled against him there was no response to my move toward intimacy. Now that Frank is gone, my recollections of our early years sometimes overwhelm me, and I sit out in the screened lanai, listen to the birds, smell the fragrance of my flowers, and do mental snapshots of the good times while Kitty curls up in my lap. A woman can only go just so far before she needs to have someone put something back into her life instead of her pouring out all the time. At least I can see that. In fact, I realize that was my need. Back then I was drained of energy and emotionally parched. I robotically went through the steps of each day just to meet my husband's special needs. Some days there were no words spoken by either of us. He couldn't hold an intelligent conversation, nor could he think in coherent thoughts, so he remained silent. Many times, even though I wanted to communicate, I didn't speak because Frank would take everything I said and twist it around and misunderstand it and have an emotional upheaval. It was so nerve-racking that, as I look back on it, it's a wonder I'm still sane.

Am I sane, Lord? Have I lost my sense of balance when it comes to the important things of this existence? Is that why I'm having this youthful exuberance over this new man in my life? Where am I headed? Are You pleased with me? Have I made more of this relationship with Bill than I should? Am I trying to ease the pain of my loss by overwhelming myself with the attention Bill is giving me? Please help me understand.

I'll put my head on the pillow, but I know I won't go to sleep easily. My mind is a rush of wondering thoughts. Even so, I'm going to try to get some rest.

Ah, a bright morning. Sleep wasn't bad. In fact, I believe I even dreamed of Bill, and it was good. He asked me to show him the way to the Savior. Now, that's a dream I want to see fulfilled.

Yes, today is a new day. When I swung my legs out from under the covers and sat up, I was hit with the idea that I would write in this journal and think practically. I've determined to write my thoughts in a way that will bring some semblance of balance into my life. I want to see everything through new eyes. If I can only step back far enough from my feelings to really see clearly, then I'll be able to make logical decisions about where to go from here.

Please help me do that, Father.

OK. Here I go.

Here is Bill, a man who is so loving, so giving, and so caring that I'm like an emotional sponge, soaking up every nuance of sweetness. I want him to hold me and caress me. With a voice as smooth as butter, he whispers unbelievable love words into my ear. His warmth is so far beyond what I could have imagined that I'm ready to melt every time we're together. I couldn't have designed a better partner for me. Not only is he loving and kind, but he's intelligent and talented. He's full of energy that radiates into my soul.

I'm going to reread the paragraph I just wrote and analyze it.

I want to answer some questions. What's happening to me? Is it right to feel this way? Should I expect more? I'm laughing at my questioning mind. Since I'm being so practical, I'm afraid this pink bubble will burst and I'll come tumbling down to earth again. Until that happens, I'm going to float on this cloud of ecstasy.

Lord, only You can make it all either go away or ...

I don't want it to go away, so I don't know what to pray.

I'm attempting to think back, to see if I've ever been at a point where I was speechless in my prayer life. As far as I can remember, no time like this has ever happened to me. This isn't working. I can't seem to step back far enough to get out of this enraptured state of mind to understand what a woman of my age should do. OK, I'll continue to try. I'm attempting to remain focused on my spiritual life, but I also sense that if my physical being is not fulfilled, then everything will be topsy-turvy. It's like the missionaries tell us, they have to first feed the physical people in those poor villages before they can feed their souls with spiritual food. Does it even make sense to use that analogy? Am I trying too hard to justify my feelings for Bill? I've got to get a grip. When I got up this morning with determination to write from a more practical standpoint, I had no idea the mental tumult I'd have to face. Being practical about something that is so irrational is nearly impossible.

I just had to sit back and breathe deeply. Now my mind is clear. At least I think my mind is clear. Okay, I think that I'm deliberating rationally, I have to look at my motives and ask myself some tough questions. Funny, as I thought about asking myself these tough questions, I had the instant thought that added, *But am I willing to answer those questions truthfully, or will I lie to myself?* I don't really know the answer. Even so, I'm willing to regroup and begin the questioning again. My thoughts clicked to a verse out of the Bible that says something about "deceiving their own selves." Hmm. I'll have to look that up to discover what it's talking about. I certainly don't want to deceive myself … or do I? Does deceiving myself appease my trepidation? I don't know.

My first question on the list is whether I'm on the verge of narcissism. (Where did that come from?) I wasn't planning on putting that question on the list, especially not at the top of the list. The thought just popped out. I've even had to look up *narcissism* to be certain I fully understand what it means. It's a lot like egoism, someone taken up with their own needs, especially physical (even sexual) needs. The first thing off the top of my head is that I am not a narcissist. I can easily justify that answer. I've never been one to put myself forward. I've never wanted to be the center of attention. I experienced all the attention I wanted, or needed, when I was a New York model and found it to be empty and hollow. Although, as a young woman, I was hit on by both males and females in the business, I never indulged in anything that could even be slightly construed as cheating on my husband. And as far as sexual fulfillment is concerned, back then I believe Frank and I had a normal relationship.

Outside our home, my job as a model gave me a life where I was the object of everyone's attention, and it was less than fulfilling. That starlit life everyone thinks is so glamorous leaves a lot to be desired. When the runway lights go dim and the flashes from the photographers stop, the emptiness makes many models fall into depression. Going from all that glitz and the bright lights to an empty apartment with barely enough light to check out her darkened image in the bathroom mirror is like a fall from heaven to the pit. That's when drugs or alcohol become appealing. A girl will use anything to make the loneliness go away. As much as it's hyped, that's no life at all; at least it wasn't for me. I discovered a fulfilling life is found in giving to others, not taking. I once heard that making a living is measured by what we get. Making a life is measured by what we give. Giving adds brightness to my life. Even back in New York I determined to be a giver.

Yes, I was tough when it came to the business end of my life but a cream puff in every other area. Because of that,

I'm having a difficult time trying to sort out my emotions through all this affection. Bill is so doting that I'm eating it up because it's genuine. His attention has so much depth to it. It's a lot different from the shallow attention I got as a model. That was superficial. People gave me attention back then in order to get what they wanted out of me. But Bill gives me attention that has meaning. He's meeting my every need. I'm so in love with him.

Wait a minute. I just read what I put on this page. I've flipped back through this diary to see if I've written *I'm so in love with him* before this entry. No, there are no earlier entries like this. Oh dear, I did say we loved each other, but this last declaration has passion in it. It's far deeper than anything I've admitted. For the life of me I didn't mean to write those words. They just flowed out of my pen.

Lord, I need Your help … again.

There I go, once more. I've gotten away from the original purpose of the entries I wanted to make today. I asked myself one simple question, and that took me on a journey into la-la-land as usual. I've got to get it together. Either I'm going to plunge into a deep relationship with this knight in shining armor, or I'm going to have to see a psychologist. This is becoming a mental, emotional, and spiritual labyrinth that has taken me on a twisting, gaping chasm of hallways and doors opening into places I'm wondering if I should venture. I have so many reservations about how far this relationship should go that I sometimes think it should end.

I just laughed out loud. It's pathetic. I'm pathetic. I laughed because this is the way I think when I'm away from Bill, but when we're together I have almost no reservations. At those moments I'm not confused and have no sense of dismay about us taking it deeper. Maybe I need to put our relationship through a test. I grunt at that thought because I feel I'd fail any testing that might keep me from his arms. But, oh, here I go again; he isn't a Christian, and that's important. It's been such a short time since we met.

You know, Lord, a lot has transpired in the blink of an eye. What should I do?

I've waited to see if I can sense God's voice in my spirit. I don't feel a thing. God is silent. I'm seriously considering putting a halt to the progression of our relationship. I don't want us to get so involved that ... Oh, who am I kidding? Even as short as our relationship has been, I'm stuck. My emotional and physical needs are far too greedy to allow me to walk away. I'm in this body, and it has urges. Does that border on narcissism? No, I don't think it does. At least, I hope it doesn't. I'm simply a thinking person, and my mind has to find stimulation. I don't understand how the human persona inside each body has emotional needs and that fulfillment of those cravings is important, but I know it's the truth. Some women may not have the same urgency, and others may deny their baser desires, but I'm a woman in need. To separate my fleshly wants from my spiritual needs is disconcerting. What a battle. It's raging inside me. I'm too old for this. Why can't I just grow old gracefully and do my volunteer work and be done with it? The answer is simple. I have desires for love and affection that are yet unfulfilled, and I'm in contact with a man who has the ability to fulfill them. Yet I sense something deep within my soul that says I should slow down. Again, I'm fighting with those feelings because of what I've been taught compared to the reality I'm living. I mean, if God is in this relationship, and He put us together, and He knows my weaknesses, then why shouldn't I go with what I yearn for? (I'm near tears as I reread what I just wrote.) *Lord, what is happening to me? Do You care? Now that was a silly question, Lord. I know You care about what happens to me. I trust in You and need Your help. Please give me clear guidance.*

Several days have passed. I'm eager to write.

I have no particular reason for feeling such anticipation this morning, but I really want to see what transpires today. That's especially true because my last entries in this diary didn't yield what I had planned. In fact, as I reread them, I see a confused woman in anguish over her lack of dedication to godly principles and yet so deeply in love that she can't seem to take control of the situation. I'm desperately asking myself, *Is that really me?*

This morning I got up a bit earlier than usual and straightened the house. I even vacuumed before dawn. After that I sat with my coffee and dreamed and prayed about this romance. Kitty pushed her way into my world and took her place on my lap. As I talked to the Lord, I got real with Him. Once again, I admitted that my emotional and physical needs were about to overwhelm me, and I asked His forgiveness for ... I'm going to say it ... *not caring* if it's wrong. Ouch! That stung. I mean I haven't *done* anything wrong, just considered it. But I thought of Jesus telling His followers (of which I am one) that it isn't the act that is so important, it's the idea that we harbor in our minds that's bad. Why? Well, I'm assuming the Lord meant that we can easily see that the actual act is wrong, but we can gloss over our thought life— since nobody knows our deepest longings. All right, so God does know. I'm also aware of the fact that He said, "If a man lusts after a woman in his heart, he has already committed the actual act." Ouch again! It's not that I don't care about my soul. I do. I care about right and wrong, and about my relationship with God. But I have to admit that my yearnings are so powerful that fulfillment of them is trying to push me beyond whatever that point is that I've been taught is forbidden. Convincing myself to do the right thing is difficult when I'm with Bill. Here, sitting on the side of the bed as I make entries into this journal, it's easy to make proper choices. However, my mind is always playing with thoughts that lead to a deeper relationship with Bill. I know that God's Word tells me to "bring into captivity every thought." Talk about hard to do. That's the most difficult of tasks. But that's what I've been taught that I must do in order to please God. And, that's not just some minister teaching me these principles. It's actually our of God's Word. Yes, I'm using an excuse by saying "what I've been taught" as opposed to what I *know* is right or wrong. I can differentiate between the two, but I'm still trying to skate by the obvious, so I won't have to consider the fact that I'm the responsible party in this relationship. After all, I'm the Christian, the one who's been made free in Christ, the one with her spiritual eyes open. That places the onus on my shoulders. If I take this relationship too far, I certainly can't blame it on Bill or on God. Bill is going with his natural instincts. God, on the other hand, has given me clear directions about controlling myself. It's up to me to take control. But how?

Maybe I got up too early this morning, and I'm still a bit hazy in my brain. The coffee is good, and I'm truly blessed with the many treats that give me pleasure. But I'm alone, a widow, old in years and young at heart. Add to that the fact that Bill is energetic, romantic, physically healthy, and (more importantly) *available*. He's everything I ever wanted in a man.

This morning my mind raced back to what Pastor

Hassler taught us in our most recent Bible study. He spoke about Paul's "thorn in the flesh." He explained that most people think of it as a weakness in Paul's body. But the Bible doesn't use that term. Paul doesn't write "a thorn in *my* flesh"—rather, "a thorn in *the* flesh." We've all used that term, "I wanted to see him, and suddenly there he was in the flesh." So, it appears Paul may have had an actual person (someone in the flesh) who was either bugging him or maybe even tantalizing him to sin. That seems especially true since Paul referred to this being as "a messenger from Satan, sent to beat me and keep me from being too proud." Pastor said that any of us who ride that wonderful spiritual high for a long period of time sometimes get proud and feel that we're above sin. I can relate. The apostle Paul tells us that he asked God three times to take away this messenger of Satan, but God's response was always the same. God said, "My grace is enough for you. When you are weak, my power is made perfect in you."

Lord, I'm so weak when it comes to my relationship with Bill that I want to run away, because I know that I can't hold out much longer. Is Your grace going to rescue me? If I fail and succumb to my feelings, will Your mercy cover my failure?

I thought about His grace and mercy and was reminded of something Joyce Myer said when speaking of her good traits. She said, "I'm quick to repent." I love that statement. But when I consider it in the context of my romance, I get the feeling that I'd use that as an escape mechanism in order to go ahead and cross the line with Bill, and then quickly repent. I know Joyce didn't mean that as a license to sin, but I've sure considered plunging head on into this relationship and then repenting quickly. Is that normal for a committed Christian? I wish I had someone in whom I could confide. The people I know are all so "churchy" that any one of them would condemn me if I explained how I feel—even though we've heard teachings on James 2:8 about the "royal law" that commands that we love one another. In our church (as they say), it ain't happenin'. Nobody seems to have that kind of genuine love for others. If they even thought I was on the verge of going to be with Bill, they'd kick me out and run me out of town.

Did I just write that I've been thinking of going to be with Bill? What am I doing? I don't remember considering hopping between the sheets with him. In fact, if I know my heart and my actions, I've done just about all I can to keep from it. Sure, I've desired it at times. Even so, I haven't *blatantly* considered it. Have I? I'm asking myself more questions than I am giving myself answers.

The thought just zapped me and made me ask, if the situation were reversed, would I be able to listen to another woman going through this and not condemn her. If another woman in our church approached me and asked me to go to lunch with her, and she told me she and an unmarried deacon were having a fling, could I fulfill the royal law and love her without judgment? I don't know. There I go, kidding myself. Before Bill came into my life along with this struggle he's put into me, I'd be just as condemning as anyone in our church. I would have turned my back on her. I'm near tears as I admit my failure to love others as Jesus loved us all.

Oh my, I've got to stop writing. I'm feeling more condemned as I enter my thoughts. This is not something I planned. It's just happening. I'm going to bed early, just to get away from it. I pray I can get to sleep quickly. If I don't I'll toss and turn and conjure up all kinds of senarios.

When I put this journal down last evening, I was frustrated. Things are different now. Bill called, and we got so involved in conversation that I didn't even think about last night's turmoil. I love to hear from him. He soothes my aching mind. In fact, waiting for his first call each morning is like a child anticipating cotton candy at a carnival. Then the phone rings, and his soft words are something like, "I hope you had a good night's sleep." He's so positive, so reassuring, and very sweet.

Today when I awakened with that same urgency to hear his voice, I realized this was all happening much too fast. I don't really know Bill. Or do I? Then I looked into the bathroom mirror as I awaited the hot water. I noted the wrinkled old lady staring back at me and reasoned that it didn't matter whether I knew every little detail about him. I dipped my cupped hands into the hot water and splashed my face. I lived with Frank for all those years and sometimes felt I didn't really know him all that well; even before he began his fade into Alzheimer's.

I realize one thing. I don't have a lot of time left on this earth. That's why I've been going through these mental gymnastics. On one hand, I've concluded that waiting and taking it easy is the best way to go forward. Then I rationalize that this is a romantic fling—at my age—and I need to go with it. I spoke to myself as I peered at my reflection in the foggy mirror. I concluded, "My lady friends will be jealous, envious, and even try to take Bill from me." I gave my image a twisted grin and used the towel to clear the mist from the glass. "What they don't know won't hurt them. I caught him, and I'm keeping him." I winked at my image.

My mental rehearsal and journal entry of this early morning heart-to-heart talk with myself was interrupted when the phone rang. I wanted to snatch it up and tell

Bill to come over and hold me close. Instead, I swallowed another sip of coffee and waited for the third ring before I picked up.

His tender voice was like warm chocolate oozing its way into my mind. The endorphins leapt to attention. I felt the rush. His sweet words invigorated my entire being. Even so, I determined to be rational and practical and even steadfast in my resolution. It was time to bring this relationship down to a slow, measured crawl. It took every ounce of resistant fiber I had, but early into our conversation I said, "We haven't known each other long enough yet, and we're calling each other like we were infatuated school kids. I think we need to put the brakes on this, because I really just want to get to know you as a friend." Ouch! Did I lie to him? Was I kidding myself?

Oh, Lord, where are You in all of this?

He seemed to take it in stride and answered, "Sweetheart, don't friends call each other?"

"Yes," I had to admit.

"Don't friends enjoy each other's company?"

I agreed.

"Then why shouldn't we take our friendship a little deeper and see what takes place?"

I pulled in a long, slow breath. What would be his definition of a *deeper* relationship? Was he doing a sales job on me? Was I being manipulated?

Lord, help! Give me the right words.

I finally responded. "Well, I have a problem with taking our acquaintance to another level until I'm sure that the level we're dealing with at the moment is on solid footing."

"Tell me what disturbs you about this thing you're calling an *acquaintance*. Have I been harsh or uncaring?"

I didn't even have to think about my answer and blurted, "*No!* Ah, no. You've been wonderful."

"Then what have I done?"

"It isn't what you've done as much as who you are and who I am." I could hear his chuckle on the other end.

"Me Tarzan. You Jane," he affirmed.

I laughed, but quickly recaptured my serious tone. "Now don't become upset with me. I'm not trying to shove anything down your throat. But you know a while back we talked about our faith, or lack of it, and you said you didn't believe in God."

His voice changed to scholarly professionalism. "It wasn't quite that chiseled in stone. I believe I said I wasn't *certain* there was a God who created all this and watches over it."

I wanted to tell him my true feelings, so I said, "Bill, I don't think I could have a relationship with anyone who didn't love the Lord. I'm a committed Christian, and the person I want in my life has to be someone who feels like I do."

Was I kidding myself? In this short courtship (if I may call it that), I felt a pang of embarrassment over my physical attraction. My body tingled when I lay awake in the dark of night, alone in my bed, wanting Bill at my side. I've been telling him what a committed Christian I am, yet I harbor desires that seem to be far from my faith. "The lust of the flesh" comes to mind. I'm in total agony. How could I say all the right words about being a devout Christian and then secretly nurture the craving to give him my all? I think that using the Christian title is a terrible misnomer when I'm not thinking like one. Or am I? Do other women in my situation want to be held, kissed, and romanced like this? Do they have the battle I'm having over their spiritual side and their human yearnings? I agonize when I consider the possible outcome.

We cut our conversation short. I concluded that Bill

really does believe in God, but he's angry with our Creator. It stems from the fact that his father died while Bill was just sixteen, and he had to drop out of school to go to work to help with family needs. He recollected his mother asking God, "Why?" She never discovered the answer to that question, and he dismissed God as a figment of his mother's imagination. That's his problem. He couldn't deal with the heartbreak his mother felt over the loss of his father, so he masked his pain with an attack against the concept of God. If he could dismiss God, he could then dismiss the pain by rationalizing all of life with the impression that things *just happen*. That way he can determine that no supernatural power exists, and therefore what happens in this life is the end of all things. No need to look for another life or "hereafter." Eternal life doesn't exist in his mind.

As for my dilemma, well, I'm trying to discuss it with myself in this journal, so that I can sort out the actual problem and conclude what the answer might be. Contrary to Bill, I'm continually looking to God for help and for answers. I have twinges of remorse for the mental images I harbor of loving this man and being loved by him. Then I disregard those misgivings and dream that dream, bathing myself in a mental slide presentation that gives me so much pleasure that I can't describe it. Should I continue to see Bill, or should I cut this relationship off before we go so far there's no turning back? I'm at my wit's end. On one hand, I can understand his anger against God. On the other hand, I wonder if I could live with him—I mean live with his lack of faith. He's a good, compassionate, and loving man. When I volunteer at the care center, he spends part of each day helping me. Every day is a challenge for him to make me laugh when I want to cry over the distorted lives of those with whom I must deal. Bill lightens the load on my mind. He's funny, and I find that so attractive. He can discover humor in just about everything. One day, while we were talking about finances and tax time, he said, "I'd never want to be an accountant." When I asked why, he said, "Because even if you never commit a crime, as an accountant you're still deemed a *person of interest*." He's always looking for a play on words. I have to intentionally be aware of the double entendre. And it makes me sharper. It isn't that witless, slapstick stuff, but true humor. It's when we're laughing or groaning at one of his puns that I feel like I've known Bill my whole life. I also have physical sensations that I haven't experienced in many years. I want him to hold me close, perhaps even make love to me. Oh, my, did I just admit that on paper again? I did. I've alluded to it before, but this time I really admitted it with conviction. It just flowed out of my fingertips on its own. Oh well, I'm being very honest here, and I'm admitting I want a physical union with this man. Somehow I hesitate to take that step. It's something that would please me, and I know he wants it too. But there's an unseen barrier that prevents it. Maybe I'm unaware that I send signals to him to keep his distance. No, no, no. It's not that I'm unaware of it. I hate to admit I'm sending those signals, because I don't want to admit that I'm scared to death of the commitment such physical contact implies. So, I signal him to back off. At those times I can see the frustration on his face, but he honors my body language. Our friendship is so precious that I'd hate to lose it. Then again, I'm struggling with my Christian values as I try to understand what God wants for me. How can I be Christ-like and still love this man who is opposed to my faith? Well, maybe I've overstated that. He isn't actually *opposed* to my faith, he just doesn't share it. I want him to be part of this wonderful relationship with God, but he's determined to stay his distance in that segment of our relationship as well.

I'm constantly reiterating in my mind that if I divulge any of this to some of my churchy friends, they'd demand that I stop seeing him. Why do I always refer back to those of my church? It's like they have a hold on my life. I guess that really bothers me. Even though most of the people I call friends are really only acquaintances, I still don't want them to reject me because of how I feel about Bill. So, to ease my conscience I've concluded that it's no one else's business, and that's that. Even so, my struggle seems to overwhelm me at times. However, God's Word tells me He won't put anything on me beyond my ability to handle. That verse of scripture really puzzles me. I know the Word of God is the purest truth, but it just seems impractical at times. It seems that I'm trying to justify my feelings so I can give in to my physical urges and have a sexual encounter with Bill. There, I've made it clear.

Now what, Lord? I've written it because I've felt it. I can't hide it from You, so what's the use in not telling it like it is? After all this is just between You and me. Am I such a bad girl that You're going to give me a spanking for feeling such passion? What am I to do? Lord, I love You and want to serve You with all my heart, but You also know my needs in this human existence. I guess what I'm facing appears to be a test of my will *or Yours being done.*

Oh boy, am I in trouble.

Our Impending Demise

e're having dinner tomorrow, and Bill told me today that after dinner tomorrow evening we need to have a serious talk. He's never seemed so grave or given his words that much emphasis. This is a new side of Bill for me. Although I too have been thinking we need to have a thoughtful talk, I wasn't prepared for this sudden confrontation. I'm afraid I'll have to make a decision as to whether to continue seeing him or not. My mind is really tumbling with one assumption over the other to figure out what he may want to talk about. I hope he isn't going to give me an ultimatum. I'm still going through too much struggle with my feelings of right and wrong to have to face a Rubicon like that. If he presses me for a decision to go on or to go our separate ways, I have no idea what I'll say. A thought just shot through my mind. *Whatever decision I make, I'll regret.* Oh no, I hope that isn't the truth. I don't want to dwell on such a negative concept. I've always been quite positive in my approach to life's conflicts.

As I reflect on the danger Bill faced in the murky Gulf waters at night and how he was rescued, I have to believe God scooped him out of the waters to save him for me. I'm laughing, because that seems so irrational—even school girlish. It makes me question my mental balance.

Does God answer prayer so far in advance of the actual need? As I read the scriptures, I find that He answered the prayer of Abraham and Sarah some fifteen years before the actual birth of Isaac. He says He'll answer even before we ask. That's how far back the promise of a son born to Sarah was given by God. So, yes, I suppose He does set up our lives well in advance. I'm smiling at myself right now and thanking God I don't have to be one of those Bible scholars who seems to have all the answers. I'm glad I'm not really certain of how God works out His plans for our lives. Even if He doesn't set things up far in advance, I'm going to cling to my hope that He put Bill into my life so that my needs will be met and that Bill will come to know Him and His saving grace. As I ponder it, I realize that isn't practical as the world sees practicality. And do I need to be practical? I actually want to be. Yet my romantic side tells me to *live the dream*. I can do nothing else but trust that my Lord has His hand in all that's happening. I believe that. I truly believe it. I'm not just blowing smoke in order to appease my guilty pleasure of romancing this nonbeliever. My inner self says that God is in this and that the way I live my life in front of Bill will ultimately bring him to the Lord. Whoa! What a load has just been put on my spiritual shoulders. Bill's eternal existence depends on my following the leading of the Lord with preciseness. But am I able to live that pristine Christian existence so that Bill will be drawn to what I have deep in my spirit? Then again, should I live above who I really am and lead him to believe that the Christian life is simple to live? I mean, Christ died to take the punishment for my sin, not to make me above sin. I know that everyone has something in his or her life that isn't right on target. And sin is missing the target. So, it is the punishment for my sin that Jesus took on Himself, not making me some robotic being when I accept what He did on the cross. I still have a free will to make choices. The difference for me is that becoming a Christian opened my spiritual eyes to allow me to make proper choices.

It's odd that I was hit with a verse out of Philippians this morning. I've read it many times, but this morning it took root. That happens to me at times. This verse was chapter one, verse 27. The apostle Paul is writing and says, "Just one thing. Live in a manner that is worthy of the gospel of Christ." That's a heavy thought. Have I ever lived such an exemplary life as to be "worthy of the gospel of Christ"? I'm doing a mental check of my life and realize what a daunting task I face if I'm to live in such a manner that Bill is drawn to a relationship with Jesus. The biggest problem is that I'm wrestling with my lust for this hunk. OK, he's an elderly hunk, but still a hunk in my eyes. What if I give in to my physical desires? Will that blow the deal? Will God have no chance to enter into Bill's life if I profess to be a totally dedicated Christian and then give in to the baser feelings of life? I have to pray. That's the only reality—deeper prayer.

Lord, I need Your help. You brought us together, of this I'm certain. What's the next step? Please lead me.

I'll miss Bill terribly if I have to stop seeing him and hearing from him. I'll miss the laughter we both have experienced. I'll miss his friendship; especially his hugs and kisses. Oh, those kisses. We have progressed from lip touching into deep kissing. The last time we were together his hot breath was around my neck and he was kissing me there in a way I've never experienced. It was so sensual that I could feel a powerful magnetic force pulling me to him. He wants more, and so do I. Will I kid myself by wondering if I'm ready for that commitment? My background is very conservative, and this new thing about a woman having the right to determine the fate of her own body is far afield from what I'm used to. Oh, there can be no pregnancy, so that's not the issue. It's just that these days women seem to be so carefree about sexual matters because they're able to have abortions for errors in judgment, or they're on the pill and have massive amounts of protection. They appear to be so casual about the life within them. And, of course, it seems to me that no one below the age of forty appears to care about moral values. At least not the deep-seated moral values I'm used to. It seems they feel there are no absolutes, no moral code, and no God with whom we all will give an account. The younger group appears to forget there is a Creator and that there will be an accounting of what was done here on earth. Now what I'm feeling is not altogether true. I can't blame it on the under-forty age group. Even the retirement villages in Florida are known for their overt sexual promiscuity. It isn't limited to the young firm-fleshed generation. And evidence that the AARP (formerly, American Association of Retired Persons) types want to be young and into the modern lifestyle is displayed by the tattoos and piercings older women now sport. Thinking of AARP, they even carried an article about the "best sex" is yet to be ours as we age. Maybe that's fine, but where does the marriage stance come into the picture? Sure, the youthful lifestyle is fun, and freedom at the cost of morality is appealing to the deep desires of my sinful self. But because of my beliefs and my moral upbringing, I'm fighting this battle. (I snickered at that thought.)

Lord, am I losing the battle? Am I?

I really do want to win at this game of life, and I want to spend eternity with my Lord and Savior Jesus Christ. Why am I even battling? Aren't I supposed to be a winner in Christ? Aren't I supposed to be strong in the power of the

Holy Spirit? Then what in the world is happening to me? Oh my, I can relate to Paul's message in Romans, chapter seven about doing what my spiritual self really doesn't want to do and planning on doing those things that are earth-driven. I too cry out to God for deliverance from this body of death. I'm a mess. My state of mind is exacerbated by what I see all around me. I mean, everybody's doing it. Why not me? Why don't I just let go and enjoy the fullness of Bill's love?

This is funny. I relax in the early evenings with the news, and I watch my favorite show, *Wheel of Fortune*. On this particular show a young female contestant said, "I live in Manhattan with my wife." It was so casual a comment that no one seemed to notice. Pat Sajak didn't flinch or acknowledge the trend toward immoral behavior. It all just flowed as though living with her girlfriend as though they are a married couple is right to do. But it isn't. I've got to question myself, *is it*? At least what I glean out of the Bible is that sex without marriage is not right in the eyes of God. And that's what I was taught as a young woman. I was taught to please God first. My question in general is, *Has humanity sunk so low that we accept all types of misbehavior*? Or am I on the wrong track? I'm considering that question and don't think I'm wrong, because I'm on target with what God's Word teaches. Whew! This is a real battle, a moral dilemma. And it's growing more intense. Doesn't the Word say that at the end of the age, "They won't know right from wrong"? It's happening right in front of my nose.

Wait a minute. I just reread what I wrote. I used the word *misbehavior* when I should have said *sin*. Am I falling into the trap of semantics? Did I write misbehavior instead of sin because misbehavior sounds less threatening than sin? And I want it to be less threatening because I'm drawn to misbehaving; ah, sinning. Actually, if I'm totally honest with myself, I do want to partake of what I consider to be sinful behavior. If I simply misbehave, the penalty seems much less severe than it is if I sin. My thinking is really going out there today. Paul's words out of Romans 7 invade my mind again because of the severity of what he is asking. "Who will save me from this body that brings me death?" And that's exactly the question I'm asking myself and God. My yearnings are so strong that I sense I'm fighting for my very life. When am I going to be strong enough to wage the war of my flesh and bring it into submission? I hope it's before I stand before the Lord on Judgment Day. Again, I know I'm not saved by the things I do or don't do. I'm solely saved by what Jesus did and my belief in the sacrifice He gave for me.

I stopped writing because there's the sound of a truck in my driveway.

I have to leave the computer and see who's here.

I'm back.

When I looked through the shears my mouth fell open. It was a florist's van. I answered the doorbell. The young man was smiling. "Miss Lilly?" he asked.

I guess I was sort of in a trance because he just stood there, and so did I.

He nodded as he presented me with a long white box. "I believe these are for you."

I reached out but he held them back.

An eyebrow was cocked up. "You are Miss Lilly. Aren't you?"

I could feel my brow wrinkle. If I didn't identify myself

quickly, he was going to take the box back to his van and drive off. "Yes!" I nearly shouted at him. "I'm Lilly!" He laughed. "I know it. Your gentleman friend described you perfectly." His eyebrow lowered. He scanned me from head to toe. His brow lifted again and he licked his lips. The glint in his eyes and the smirk on his lips spoke far too much. He added, "All the way down to your sensitive smile and beautiful eyes."

I was thankful that he didn't mention my legs. Bill wouldn't dare tell him about my legs.

Then I wondered if this kid was hitting on me or just looking for a bigger tip? I smirked at him and said, "Wait just a moment."

I took the box and set it on the coffee table and got a few dollars out of my purse, gave him the tip, and he left. When I opened the box, I held my breath. There ensconced in white tissue, a dozen long-stemmed red roses smiled up at me. I picked up the card. *Lilly, I simply wanted to express the beauty of life through these roses. Until tomorrow evening, Bill*

I read it and reread it. What is this message? What is he saying? The words are puzzling. Usually, a dozen roses sent to a woman suggest romance. The card with them normally is a love note. This card has no romantic lilt, no sweet nothings scribbled across it, and not a bit of love to it. This isn't the Bill I've grown to know over the few months we've been together. I mused over it and concluded that I'd have to call him and thank him for this lovely gift. Dare I ask what the meaning of this message is? I don't want to put him on the spot. But I do want to find out what he's thinking about our relationship.

The handset shook in my grip as I hit the buttons. I even wished he wasn't home to answer.

He must have been right next to his phone, maybe waiting for this call. He picked up on the first ring.

I immediately went into my prepared speech. "I want to thank you for the flowers. That was so sweet." I hesitated and added, "You really know what pleases a woman."

His response was unique. "Did I confuse you with my little message?"

Oh my, he beat me to the punch. "I'll have to be honest. You did," I admitted.

"Well, don't be too concerned. I was leaning on the counter at the florist, and the clerk was staring over my hands as I wrote. I felt ill –at ease and didn't want to really write what I felt while she looked on. So, I just wrote about the beauty of life." He chuckled. "The beauty of life is you, sweet Lilly."

I could feel my brow pull together. It didn't sound right. Even in the short time I've known Bill I'm certain he's not easily embarrassed, and he wouldn't allow some clerk to intimidate him. At least that's how I view him. It seemed there was more to this than I could see. But I let it go and repeated, "Thank you. It's a wonderful gift."

We talked a little more before we hung up. Even after we were off the phone, I pondered what might be happening. I let my mind wander through the corridors of suggestion. It led me down a long emotion-filled hall from one scenario to the next. Puzzling as it was, I continued to muse about it.

Maybe it's a woman thing, intuition or some other gift God has bestowed upon the female half of the population, but I sensed that something wasn't exactly as it seemed. At least that's what I finally concluded. Suddenly my mind went into overdrive, and the thought of *another woman* in Bill's life zapped me. I attempted to dismiss it, because it wasn't even rational, unless Bill was playing a ... I don't even want to write it or say it. If another woman has entered the picture, how could I compete, especially if she's young and pretty? Actually, if there *is* another woman, I wouldn't want to compete. I definitely don't want a man who is so sweet and tender to my face but stabbing me in the back when we aren't together. And since he isn't a Christian, I suppose anything's possible with him. I allowed myself to consider why he might want to have me on one hand and another woman on the other. He's a man. I'm only giving in to *some* of his needs, wants, and desires. Maybe he has someone else who's willing to take it to the next level and fill in the blanks. I wonder if she's pretty, shapely, and generally appealing. I heard myself grunt. I'll bet she's curvy. I caught my eyes glancing down at my chest.

Even when I was a model, I didn't like my body. In reality, modeling made me more aware of my lack of curves than I normally would have been. However, the designers didn't want a lot of hips or bust, because they wanted every model to appear slim. In modeling, slim is in, and the slimmer the better. I've always been a little edgy because of my body, but modeling heightened that sensitivity. Of course, at my age I don't expect to look like a teenager, but it's more than the age, the wrinkles, and the sagging skin. I wasn't blessed with a lot of natural curves, especially when it comes to my breasts. That was fine when I was a Manhattan model. It was in vogue then, even as it is in the modeling world today. But now, I need some meat on my bones, and it needs to be in the right places. My A-cup makes me feel less ... No, that's not the word I want to use. I feel ... Oh, phooey! I'll just say it. I'd like to have bigger boobs! Why? Because I think ample breasts are pleasing to a man. I've read the Song of Solomon and know how pleasing nice breasts are to the lover portrayed there. But I've got what I've got. Maybe it won't matter anyway, because we may never get to that depth of relationship. That's absolutely true if Bill has another woman on the string. Am I kidding myself? I don't even know anything about any other woman. It's all in my mind. Why am I beating my brains out when I don't know anything about another woman in his life? We women are notorious for hacking ourselves to death over some figment of our imagination and then allowing that image to grow into mental reality. Someone once said, "Perception is reality." I guess that's the truth. Whatever I perceive to be true makes it true in my mind, and therefore it becomes reality to me. Ooh, I hate that about myself.

I recently read about the brothers of Joseph before he had revealed his identity to them and had invited them to have a meal at his table. The brothers were contemplating why this powerful man of Egypt would invite them into his home. They surmised that he wanted to take them in and enslave them and even steal their donkeys. They had no idea what was to happen, but came up with the worst scenario. That seems to be me. Bill wants to "steal my donkeys." I'm chuckling as I consider how I always seem to come up with some outlandish concepts. I forget that God is for me, not against me. He will see that I have the best. I have rest in that understanding.

It's odd that I didn't talk to Bill concerning my feelings, and he didn't ever broach the subject that he was concerned about it either. Are we avoiding the inevitable, serious talk? As I consider how we're skirting certain aspects of our relationship, it seems neither one of us want to be first to bring it up.

Our Turmoil

I went to bed last night considering what my female competition for Bill's admiration may look like. Many pictures entered my twisted mind. I say my mind is twisted because I couldn't sleep, and the mental gymnastics turned from one scenario to the next until it was a jumbled mess. I realize that's not the way a faith-filled person is supposed to handle life's arduous trials, but I'm human for goodness' sake. I wasn't born with the ability to overcome my need for love and affection from male companionship. Being the woman I am, I yearn for closeness—especially since Frank and I lived together for the last decade without much tender touching, sweet talking, or natural husband/wife intimacy. I'm starved. I don't know how some women can make it for years without the tender touch of a man. Not only do I miss those soft touches, but I miss having a man to open jars I can't seem to budge, to step up on a ladder to hang Christmas decorations, or to ask me to rub his sore back muscles. It's those small but cherished things that I miss.

After about three hours of that kind of thinking, I finally gave up and fell asleep. Kitty was at my feet the entire time—purring her own lullaby from dreamland. I envy my precious cat. She can sleep at peace all the time because she has no worries. I provide everything for her, and she trusts that I'll continue to do so forever. Maybe that's my problem; I'm not putting my full trust in the Lord. Ouch! That thought stung. But it makes perfect sense. If I fully trusted God to work out His plans in my life, then I'd let it all go and put all my decisions in His hands. Let me think about it right here on paper. Somewhere in God's Word I've read something like, *acknowledge the Lord in everything you do, and He will give you directions.* Why don't I do that? Am I so egotistical as to think I can plan my own future when I don't even know what the next moment will bring? This is disconcerting. I truly thought I was living a life that was fully dedicated to God. But as I analyze it, I'm playing games with my own mind. Wow! A verse of scripture just zoomed across my mind. Again, it's in Romans. Paul has talked about the sins of the flesh overtaking him, and he then asks, "Who will deliver me from this body that brings on death?" Why do I keep going back to that same verse? Paul also says that he thanks the Lord Jesus Christ because, he says, with his mind he serves the law of God but with his flesh he serves the law of sin. So, the great apostle Paul was in the same turmoil I find myself in today. Maybe that's why the Holy Spirit keeps bringing that verse to mind. I need to see that I'm not alone when it comes to fighting the good fight of faith. I suppose there would be no fight of faith if there were no negatives to fight against. Now that's a two-edged sword. On one edge I feel relief that Paul too had his fight with fleshly desires. On the other edge is the fact that I'm even in this fight when I thought I was beyond such sinful concepts. Again, I see myself as a real spiritual, mental, and emotional basket case. I have to confess *that* again; *I'm a mess*! That's not a negative confession, simply the truth.

When I awakened this morning, I determined to let

go of the thought of another woman and focus on Bill and what I'm to do to please God and follow through with this … this relationship. I'm even struggling with what to call it. My mind is out of tune with the peace that passes all understanding.

Oh, Lord, I need You.

Even after I struggled to get my head on straight and thought I was missing the mark, the day went well, and Bill and I had a wonderful time together. We ate dinner at what has become our restaurant, the Pepper Mill.

He loaned me two books written by his son, who is an inspirational author. It so amazes me that Bill is against the concept of God, but his son is a deeply rooted Christian. What an enigma! How could Bill's son have a relationship with Jesus after being raised by a man who doesn't have a clue about the cross of Christ? I guess my consternation was showing, because Bill asked if something was bothering me. Of course, I didn't want to shove anything down his throat, so I shrugged it off and smiled as I turned my attention to the succulent meal before me. Remaining silent on the subject that was perplexing me is far better than causing him to be baffled as well. It wasn't that I didn't want to approach the subject of his failure to commit to Christ, I certainly wanted to. But I sensed the timing was not right and turned to much lighter subjects.

I'm going to stop entering what happened for a moment so I can write my heart in prayer. Such moments of writing out my prayers have been a great form of therapy for me. I sometimes go back and read them and pray them several times.

Father, Your Word tells me in Matthew 11:12 that we should be aggressive in our faith. Does that mean I should go ahead and get forceful about telling Bill about Your

Son? That seems to be a bit too aggressive when the man doesn't even believe You exist and that You are overseeing everything and everyone in Your vast universe. I don't want to push him away before we really have a chance to make something out of our relationship. That's especially true since I believe You are in it. Lord, I really need You to give me both wisdom and patience. If You aren't in this relationship even though I'm believing that You are, then put the words in my mouth that will either shove it down his spiritual throat so he is able to digest it, or send him on his way. Thank You for hearing and answering.

I feel better now, so I'm going to continue to write about our date.

Let me see where I was. Oh, yes, the Pepper Mill for dinner. Yum! It was delicious. An appetizer of succulent stuffed mushrooms prepared my palate for filet mignon while he enjoyed baby back ribs. Coffee afterward enhanced the most delicious chocolate-dipped strawberries I've ever tasted. At that moment I allowed my thoughts to take flight. *I wonder if it's the food that's better than average, or is something going on inside my mind (even my heart) that makes life much sweeter.* I supposed that it was God working out His will in our lives.

Oh sure, this man is not my idea of the perfect man, but he's close. The perfect man would only come in a package wrapped in Jesus. But there's so much Bill has to offer. He's vibrant, laughs a lot, and makes me laugh more than I have in many years. Along with that, he has those wonderful moments of tenderness and a gentle touch that causes time to stand still. That makes me look forward to what's coming next. I guess Walt Disney lived in a fantasyland of his own creation, and maybe that's exactly what's happening to me. Look what Walt developed out of the fantasy he carried in his mind concerning a mouse.

I've got more than a mouse to deal with. I'm going to pray more about this.

Lord, You're the Great Creator, so please make it clear. I want this to be of You, not some whipped up emotional experience of my own making.

I've discovered that I'm caught in the tangled web of two forces. Bill is as perfect as a non-Christian can be, but that's just it—he isn't a committed Christian and refuses to even talk about it. My upbringing pulls at me in the opposite direction. I wonder if it's coming from what I've been taught all those years, or am I sensing the tender nudging of the Holy Spirit to get out of this relationship.

Even as nice as Bill was at dinner, there were times during the meal that a flash of wonder about another woman hit me. I chuckled inside and dismissed it as quickly as I was able so that my mood wouldn't change and ruin a perfectly beautiful evening. However, I indulged myself and considered the fact that I wouldn't be happy until I was sure I was the only woman in his life. There would always be that question if I didn't resolve it one way or another.

I got my answer through a glimpse of the vulnerability of William Harper Carrington. It happened after coffee and that wonderful strawberry dessert. A situation arose that made me realize his humbling encounter with the florist wasn't beyond his practical, choleric nature. And from that I surmised there was no other woman for me to contend with or even be concerned about. It happened when our server came to ask if we needed anything more. We didn't, so she turned down the check, placed it on the linen tablecloth and said, "I can take this when you're ready, Mr. Carrington."

Bill glanced at the back of it, but before picking it up asked, "Are you certain you don't want anything else?" I assured him that I didn't, and our server nodded and left to visit the next table. Bill leaned to one side and reached back for his wallet. The unexpected horror in his eyes made his tanned face turn pale. Instantly, I saw little Billy Carrington come alive. I could see the shocked little boy cast a pall over his eyes. The man was no longer in control. He instantly turned into a child in trouble. This naturally poised, take-charge, powerhouse was suddenly very vulnerable. My assessment of him took an odd turn. Yes, I still respected his manly leadership nature, but I was pleased to see that he also had a chink in his armor that made him as human as the rest of us.

He didn't have to tell me that he had forgotten his wallet, it happened to my Frank once when we were in a posh restaurant in Manhattan. We were married at the time, so it was no big deal. Frank wasn't trying to impress me, and when he discovered that he'd forgotten his billfold he told me that's what had happened and asked for my credit card.

However, at this restaurant, with Bill, it was quite different. He had asked me to dinner and was supposed to pay. He too was from the old school. Asking me to pick up the check was out of the question for a man like him. I noted his helplessness and felt I had to do something and do it quickly. I reached over and picked up the check, put my hand into my clutch and pulled out my credit card. As I laid it on the check I smiled and softly said, "It's my turn. Let me get this one."

The relief on his face was priceless. "Are you sure?" he asked.

"Positive," I assured.

He swallowed hard and whispered, "I'll pay you back when we get to my place."

I waved it off.

"I want to get it," he said and then leaned across the table to whisper. "I left my wallet on the dresser in my bedroom. I can visualize it sitting there. I was putting on my jacket when I noticed it and then my watch got hung up in the coat sleeve and my attention to that made me forget the wallet."

He was rambling on from embarrassment, and I smiled. My love for him deepened at that very moment.

I waved at it again. The server ran the card and brought it back to our table. I signed the tab, added a generous tip, and we departed. Deep in my heart I was glad he had forgotten his billfold. The real man, turned little boy, came out. Doesn't every woman want a man who can be all man when the situation calls for it, but be vulnerable as well? We love men who are powerful leaders who can also show their human side—even cry at those special moments. I want that in a man. I'm amazed at how much more respect I have for him now. He's real, not some conjured up piece of manly perfection, created to woo me into ... Well, there we go again. Not a subject I want to unwrap right now.

We never said a word about the incident while we drove to the shore and sat on a beach towel to watch the late evening sun disappear into the warm Gulf waters. Although September in Florida is the middle of hurricane season and is usually hot and humid, this evening carried along some cool breezes, and I felt chilled. Bill and I snuggled. His arms wrapped around me to protect me from the night air. My heart melted. That warm sense of being protected from the elements was all I needed to fall more in love with William Carrington. He was so multifaceted and genuine that I couldn't help loving him.

I don't know what made me do it, but I mentioned that I was keeping a journal.

"You mean like tracking the hurricanes this season?" he asked.

He didn't have a clue that it was this love account. I glanced up. He was smiling. I smiled too. "No. Not a hurricane tracking chart."

A slight frown pulled at his forehead and then his brow lifted.

I pulled my gaze away and scanned the distant horizon. "Just a journal," I posed.

He squeezed my shoulders and asked, "Come on. What kind of journal?

My thoughts ran together as I wondered why I even mentioned it. I didn't know what to say. I'd really stuck my foot in it. This time it was evident that I'd be the vulnerable one. I sighed and waved a hand as though it was some trivial matter. "Ever since we met there seemed to be something special about our relationship and I decided to keep a ... a ... diary about how we ..." I wanted to use the right words. If I said we had a *friendship* that would convey coolness toward our bond, but if I used *romance* to describe what we shared, it would convey something so much deeper, and I wasn't sure how he'd react to that. Then, I considered if I was I ready to let him know that I had fallen in love with him. Oh, the struggle going on inside me was wearing me down. This agony kept me from blurting it out.

Instead of answering him I resorted to feminine (I hate this word) manipulation and asked him to hold me closer. "I really feel a chill." His face was against mine and I turned toward his ear and whispered, "Let me just say that I'm keeping a diary about our time together and the fun we're having."

Thank you, Lord.

That answer was a God thing for sure.

He nodded and smiled sweetly.

We continued to stare out at the burnished sky as the last remnants of that big orange ball disappeared into the dark waters. His lips were near my ear. Those tender words flowed like warm honey into my hearing. "Lilly, you're the sweetest woman in the world. From the moment we met, I too felt we had something very special to share." He hesitated as though he may be gathering his thoughts. "I've been writing a journal of sorts as well. It's not a diary from day to day, rather a few entries about the special moments we've had together. You know. Those times we may want to remember when we sit out on the lanai and reminisce." He was talking to me, yet it appeared he was telling *himself* how he felt. Now, his chin lifted and he placed it on the top of my head as I leaned my cheek against his chest. He directed his words heavenward. "You've been sent into my life as an angel. You're a spark of light that makes me dream of a happy future. At night I lie in bed picturing you. I see your face, so beautiful." He pulled his chin back and peered at me from the side. "I haven't told you that your presence has the effect of an elixir of youthfulness that transports me back to a time when innocence prevailed." He smiled. "You're like a virgin goddess. Yet there's an underlying spark of adventure pulling me into your web."

"My web?" I laughed. "So, you think I'm a black widow."

"Not really. More like a vixen."

"Oh, a female fox? I suppose you'll be saying I'm *foxy*."

We laughed unabashedly as darkness slowly covered the beach. The soft splashing waves caressed the shoreline. The predictability of their cadence was comforting. I was getting a bit chillier and Bill held me as close as he could. He whispered, "You know there's a hurricane forming in the Caribbean." He added, "But the churning in that torrent is no match for the stir you've created in me. My very soul is on fire with desire for only you."

I'll admit that his poetic side has me dazzled. He knows how to make my heart sing.

I nuzzled against his chest and moaned. After a deep breath I turned my face up to gaze directly into his eyes. "You make me feel like I'm so young and beautiful."

He smiled. "You are young and beautiful."

I locked my eyes on his and whispered, "Thank you."

He softly sang, "You're so young and beautiful, and I love you so. You're lips so red. You're eyes that shine shame the stars that glow. So fill these lonely arms of mine and kiss me tenderly. Then you'll be forever young and beautiful to me."

Although he didn't have the voice of Elvis Presley, Bill's melodic baritone brought goose bumps to my arms. I was enthralled. This was my earthly heaven.

I was genuinely thankful. Only God could have put this man in my life. Only the Lord knew I needed this kind of affection. Here was a man who could give me poetry, sing love songs into my ear, and even cook meals that tantalized my palate.

I turned back to watch the last remnants of orange haze fade into black over the distant waters as he continued humming the tune. We sat in the darkness and took in the feeling of each other's warmth.

He stopped humming and whispered, "You'll always remain young and beautiful to me."

I didn't respond verbally, but snuggled even closer and felt the warmth of his body; his arms wrapped around me so tightly. It was a time of snuggling I never wanted to end. But I knew it had to. It was getting much too cool for us, and there was increasing moisture in the air. We didn't want to get caught in one of those Florida instant downpours.

About ten minutes after sitting in total darkness, we left the beach and drove to Bill's home. The first thing in the door he went to his bedroom and got his wallet. "Here," he said, "let me give you this." He handed me the money to cover the restaurant check and the tip.

"You didn't need to pay me back," I assured.

He chuckled. "I don't want you to think I'm after you for your money."

I had to chuckle and make comment. "If that's what you're after, you'll be sorely disappointed."

We both laughed.

He poured two elegant stemmed glasses of Chardonnay, and we slowly sipped as we sat on the sofa and talked. During one moment when our conversation was transfixed into a lull of deep concentration Bill held me close, my head resting on his shoulder. His gentle kiss on the top of my head was heartwarming. It made me smile. His strong arms around me felt good. It was as though we picked up our beach hugs right there on the sofa. When I turned my gaze up to look into those deep blue eyes, his lips brushed mine. Then he kissed me like I have never been kissed. His lips lightly pressed against one corner of my mouth, not on my lips, yet on the edge of my mouth. That off-center kiss stirred me. I wondered, *How did he know such a lopsided kiss would cause me sensual palpitations? Is Bill more of a worldly man than I had imagined or than he let on?* I shook those concerns from my overtaxed brain and enjoyed the moment. It was so warm and inviting.

As my natural senses heightened, the spiritual side of me flashed a warning sign. Before I got too carried away, my guardian thoughts were trying to get my attention. I heard him moan and I pressed my anxiety down and away. I wanted to take pleasure in this moment and refused to allow my spiritual inclinations to deter me. Yet my Christian upbringing forged ahead. I was in love, there was no doubt. But to fulfill that attraction with submission would be too much, too soon. Even so, I savored the tantalizing sensations. The recall of my pastor reminding the congregation that, "We all want to send sin packing, but we don't want it to go too far away," was now a reality. The lure of Bill was so enticing.

His lips easily slid across my mouth to gently caress the other side—still off-center. That tingling in my lower stomach radiated down into my thighs. Finally, when I felt I could stand it no more, Bill kissed me with parted lips. I received his deep kiss. All at once passions in me that had been latent for eons came to life. All my resolve to hold back melted away. I became aggressive and pulled him so close I thought I might crush my tiny bosom. His hands slid across my back. He pulled me to him. Oh, I wanted more. I wanted him to take me, ravish me, and even devour me in his passion.

Again my faith and my background surged forward. I eased back and moaned. "Just hold me," I pleaded. "Please, just hold me." He nibbled on my neck, and I raised my chin to allow him full access. I opened my mouth so that I could breathe deeply. I had to take a moment to gather my senses. Some far away warrior princess stood up inside me and demanded I conquer my archaic inhibitions. But my rational mind overwhelmed my need to have Bill to the fullest. Here we were, a couple of AARP members acting like we were Phi Beta Kappa pledges fulfilling vows to rid ourselves of our virginity in order to become part of the college-in-crowd. What was that? I had to take a few moments to think things through.

"Bill," I whispered.

He didn't respond and kept nibbling.

I gently pushed him away.

He frowned, suddenly aware of my resistance.

I put a finger across his lips and asked, "Is it all right if we just talk?" I took my finger away.

He eased his hold on me. The unfocused gaze in his eyes slowly became cognizance, and he sighed. "If we have to." His grin told me he was ready to take our relationship to the final level.

After sucking in a deep breath, I stared at him. I knew I was ready for that commitment too, but I had obstacles to overcome and wanted to be sure this was right for us. I knew my smile was a weak attempt to appease his burning passion, so I said, "I feel like I'm on an emotional roller coaster." Our eyes were connected. "I'm very fond of you, and I want our romantic lives to be all you want. But I have issues to resolve. I need time to sort out what all this means to both of us."

That's when Bill surprised me. He didn't change his gaze when he said, "This is what I wanted us to talk about last night. We never got around to it, so we can now." He caressed my hair with the sweep of his hand. "I don't just want sex. I'm not a teenager whose hormones are out of control."

There was a tiny moment between that declaration and his next sentence. I wondered what was coming. We're finally going to reveal our true selves. Now, with him it has to do with our sexuality. But his statement unnerved me. I mean, I've always been taught that sex is all that's on every man's mind and it's the ultimate goal of every relationship a man has. Now I was curious. How was Bill going to justify the truth about men and the statement he just made? I determined to listen closely, because I figured this was going to be interesting.

He continued, "I know that when we both have what we want—that is a commitment to a long-term relationship—our sexual expression will consummate that commitment. I just want you to know that my hope is for a long-term commitment, not a tryst ending in regrets." His eyes were moist with emotion. "That's what we need to talk over. Mary was the love of my life when we were young. Our marriage was bliss. Well, not all the time, but most of the time it was wonderful. Then she got sick, and everything melted away. I'm not talking about my love and commitment to her. But any communication of substance and any intimate relationship we had experienced were gone." He swallowed, and his chin quivered slightly. "Lilly, sweetheart, you've restored life for me. I was ready to die. Like I already mentioned, I even told my daughter that I may last only a few months after Mary died." He stopped to take a deep breath, and his mouth twisted. "That was my intent. There was nothing to live for. Then you came as an apparition of loveliness that transformed my broken life into hope and restoration. Your willingness to have a meaningful conversation punctuated with humor, or concern, or even sadness for the plight of others has me hungry for more. Your eyes sparkle with life. Your lips offer me the taste of a sweet melon in peak season. Your body ..." He hesitated, grinned and bowed his head like a little boy who was naughty. Then he lifted his eyes and admitted with a mumble, "The thought of it delights my taste for the exotic." He was still grinning as his eyes penetrated my wonder. "You see, although sex is the least of my concerns, it's the culmination of all that you are to me. When we make love, it'll be the seal that solidifies our long-term commitment to each other."

It must have taken me thirty seconds to gather in his words, sort them, and process them, but when I fully understood his intentions, I was enamored and threw my arms around him. I held his head against my throat and felt him pull me to him. As he nuzzled against my neck my mind exploded at the thought of our union. His words, "although sex is the least of my concerns," really puzzled me. Was Bill just playing with words here? Could he, because of his age, really have placed his need for sex way down the list of priorities? I had to doubt that. He's a man, for crying out loud. I shook the thought and took in his embrace, never dreaming I could feel this way again—like a teenager madly in love for the first time. Bill told me that I gave him a taste for the exotic. He possessed quite an imagination. What a man.

We didn't make love, but parted that night with a tender kiss and gentle squeeze. It was wonderful. And I felt like I had pleased God. I can't wait to see Bill again. But I'll have to wait. And I know I'll have to be on guard as well. I'm very open to the lust of the flesh right now.

When I went to bed my concern about another woman was completely eradicated. I was glad I hadn't brought it up.

Kitty listened to me ramble on about the evening as she curled up on the bed at my feet. I even told her that I was becoming more like her. I too was fully trusting God to provide for everything I needed. I could get a good night's sleep because I was at peace. However, I was so excited about the future that it took a long while to come off that emotional high and actually get some needed rest.

Our Agony Apart

We spoke this morning, and Bill said, "I spend every waking moment thinking of you."

"Yes!" I nearly shouted. "And I awaken in the middle of the night calling your name."

"Do you call out for Frank too?"

"Bill," I assured him, "although I loved Frank dearly, there's no comparison. You and Frank are two very different people. Frank was a unique man. He brought joy into my life. But he's gone. Now you, in *your* unique way, bring so much more. It may be callous of me, but I've actually put my past as far back into my memory banks as possible so that I can focus on us. Is that wrong?"

"No. I don't think so. I've done the same. Today is the most important day of my life. Today is the day I'm alive and well and it's because of you. This is, as they say, the first day of the rest of my life. So, I'm overjoyed. I'd rather say that this is a new beginning for the rest of my life. I had assumed that life at this stage had nothing for me. For some reason I only saw bleak, dark days. Then, this angel appeared, and she brought with her a bright light that penetrated my soul."

"That's so sweet."

"I mean every word," he assured.

"I know you do. I can feel it. But ..."

"What? What is it?" There was a moment of silence before he added, "Don't hold back."

"Well," I began slowly, "I was curious."

"About what?"

"I don't know if I should even mention this, but I have to ask."

"Sure. Ask. Ask anything."

"Like I said, I'm just curious." I hesitated once again, then added, "Why did you mention Frank?"

I heard him chuckle before answering.

"The reason I asked if you call out for Frank is because I was lying in bed thinking of you and I felt a little guilty. I wasn't recalling memories of Mary and me and our *past life*—then for you and me there are only thoughts of us as we are together now. It's as though all we have overshadows everything I had with Mary. I believe that what we're experiencing today has erased ... Ah, no, not erased those years, but blurred them like a used eraser would do on a blackboard. All those years with her are a blur. This overpowering sense of you has taken me to this point where it's just you and me. It's as though there is no past. I can't shake this knowing that we were meant for each other at this point in our lives. I'll admit that I've *tried* to focus on just us. I guess I've done a great job of it. You see, I too have attempted to put my past way back there. I didn't really know if I had succeeded until this very moment. Then, there was always the guilt. Maybe I needed reassurance that forgetting the past was the right thing to do and you just gave me the answer. I guess I wanted to hear you say you've done the same thing. That declaration gave me a sense of truth. What I mean by that is that I felt I had been lying to myself. It could be that I was feeling guilty because of my deep feelings for you that override all the feelings I had for Mary—no, not override those feelings. Why can't I come up with the right words?" He stopped a moment, then began anew. "I guess I've push them back so far that they are totally obscure. The continual mental picture of your loveliness has taken over every fiber of my being. I suppose I wanted to know if I should feel guilty about that. You have given me assurance that what I'm experiencing is right."

I thought, *Oh my, this is beyond words. This man is saying he loves me more than life itself. And I feel the same about him.* I calmed my mind before answering. "My darling Bill, you shouldn't feel guilty," I reassured. "I feel the same way. I'm overwhelmed with this magnet of attraction that drives me. Frank and I were attracted to each other. I won't deny that. But he's gone. Your Mary is gone. Now, you can continue to make me happy, and I can satisfy your hunger for communication, a gentle touch, and companionship." I admitted, "We've become so intimate."

"We were very close a couple of times," he added.

I had to laugh a little, because he couldn't possibly know just how close we were last evening. Any more of those deep kisses and I may not have slept in my own bed. And when I did get into bed last night, it was fitful. I nearly shredded my pillow as I clutched it so tightly. Oh, how I wanted Bill at my side. But I didn't tell him any of that. Instead, I changed the direction of our conversation as I nearly blurted, "Not to change the subject." Then I lowered my voice. "But we have to." I waited for his response, but there was none, so I added, "What do you plan to do this morning?"

"The truth is I want to be with you."

I thought he was trying to continue our dream-world conversation, so I waited to hear more. He went with my inclination to leave that subject behind and move on to more substantive things, things that were relevant for the day.

He let go of our talk about our physical attraction and said, "Well, the truth is, I promised Charlie Denton that I'd go with him to take a look at the centerboard on his sailboat. We're going to be around the slip at Clearwater Beach Marina. Charlie has a case of submarine claustrophobia. He says that when he's underwater he panics and can't go more than six feet down. Swimming under the sailboat is impossible for him. It's a snap for me."

I was alarmed. "Be careful," I warned. "It sounds dangerous."

He laughed. "Piece a' cake," he scoffed. "I'm old, but I am still a strong swimmer."

"Will you be wearing scuba gear?"

"No. Just goggles so I can work on that centerboard. It's not dropping down as it should, and I think I can fix it."

I sighed. "I don't like the sound of this venture. I can't forget what you told me about your night in the Gulf. I'll worry until you've finished it and I know you're safe."

Like an old Jewish mother, I became familiar with New York, he put on the voice and assured me, "Oy vey. Not to worry. I've done it a million times on other boats."

I wanted to change the subject but had to ask, "How long will that take?"

He dropped to his normal speaking voice. "I don't know sweetheart. Maybe we'll be finished by noon."

"What do you have planned then?" I grimaced, thinking that question smacked of a clinging and confining woman who wanted to pull the strings on her puppet man. We were just dating for heaven's sake. But in my mind I sounded like a demanding married woman making her husband give an account of his life moment by moment.

Bill was free after many years as a caregiver, and I didn't want to make him feel as though I have him cuffed to my side (although that's what I really want).

"Honestly?" he asked.

"Honestly," I ventured.

"We're going to take her out and see how she sails. If it were my boat, I'd invite you to go along. Since she's Charlie's and we're actually going out to do a test run, I don't want to infringe on his—"

I jumped in. "I understand! It's all right. I want to do some shopping anyway."

That was the great thing about our relationship. Even though we wanted to be together all the time, there were moments when we showed restraint. I'll admit it was agony for me to do so, but I gave my best attempt at sounding carefree. Deep down I wanted to be with him. I mean, really be with him. But at the same time I wanted him to feel he could do his thing and I could do mine. It appeared to be tougher for me than it was for Bill. He seemed to be at ease with his new freedom. On the other hand, I was like many of the slaves when the Emancipation Proclamation abolished slavery. So many of them stayed with their slave owners because they were afraid to venture out, afraid of this freedom they had never experienced. I was so close to feeling that way. I wanted to be free, but I wanted to be loved and held and ... oh, I don't know how to explain it. Maybe I'm still a little girl inside. He interrupted my reflections.

"What kind of shopping?" he asked.

"Do you remember me telling you about Brenda Whitehall, the lady who lives down the street from me?"

He hesitated then said, "I've never met her, but I remember you mentioning her name."

"She's asked me to go to the mall with her. She has a

new grandbaby and wants me to help her pick out some things. It's going to be one of those times we women love to live. Although I've never had children, it still gives me great pleasure dressing little girls in pink. Her grandbaby is the cutest little girl."

"Good," he said. "So, we'll both be doing things that fit our gender."

I don't know who we thought we were fooling with all this free-to-be-me stuff, but my heart yearned to be with him, and I sensed that he too wanted to be with me. We were secretly subduing our agony. If we had been like many teenagers, we would have given in to those cravings. But as adults we honor commitments to others. We have our heads on straight ... Sure! Right! I can see that I'm trying to convince myself even in this diary. I'm about to cry I want to be with him so badly. I want his touch, his caress, the scent of him at my side. My need for him sometimes overwhelms me. No kisses. No whispers. No romantic contact. All I want is to have Bill hold me close while we just sit together without a word spoken. Even so, I kept silent about it and decided to go do the granny thing with my friend.

We ended our conversation by saying how much we would miss each other. And when we hung up, I leaned against the counter to pray.

God, how can this be? How have You allowed me to experience such wonderful love in the waning years of my life? These are truly the golden years for me. What seemed tarnished and rusted has been restored to newness of life. What a wonderful God You are. How many women would give up everything to have one day immersed in this love dream? Yet here I am bathing in the thought of the rest of my life lived in ecstasy with this man. Who am I, Lord, that You should bless me with a second chance at love?

Immediately I was overwhelmed with my desire to make love to Bill, to have him take me in his arms and never let go. But we aren't married, and my values tell me we have to wait. The passion setting me on fire screams to taste fulfillment.

I can't believe what's happening to me. One minute I just want to be held, and the next I'm on fire with longings I thought were dead and buried long ago. This is a battle like I've never encountered in all my Christian experience. And what I can't get over is that this is happening to me—a gray-haired old lady. I mean, I can imagine it for a woman who's still young and vibrant. But here I am, a wrinkled widow burning to have an intimate encounter with a man I'm not sure will enter into a long-term relationship. What's happening?

God, only You understand this battle raging in me. Help!

The biblical verse that says we haven't yet fought against sin until we've bled haunts me. I don't know where to find it, and I really don't want to. All I know is that it's true. I haven't bled yet in this battle of my mind and body against my spirit. But at any moment I might sweat blood because of the anguish within me. I'm fighting off my passion in order to please the Lord. Even so, He seems to be so far from me. I continually whisper, "Jesus, are You in this? Please let me know somehow." I'm in agony and ecstasy at the same time.

I have to get my mind off Bill and onto my trek to the mall with Brenda. We're scheduled to have a good time together. That's what we both said would happen. We'd shop 'til we drop. We plan to stop at the food court and get a Chick-fil-A sandwich, rest, and talk. I reminded myself that I can't talk to Brenda about Bill. If I get started describing my feelings, there's no telling how long we'd be sitting in those uncomfortable chairs in the mall's food court. I think they design those hard chairs so that shoppers will gobble their food and move on as quickly as possible to make room for others. Even with comfortable chairs, I don't think I could talk to Brenda about my feelings. She's one of those people whose been raised in the church, and she can't imagine how those of us who are still in the growing process battle our old nature. Apparently, she's never had to fight the good fight of faith or resist the devil. Either that or she's lying through her capped teeth and expecting me to believe it. Anyway, she's a good friend and doesn't ask questions about my personal life. She has to refrain from it so that we can remain good friends.

Whew! I'm worn out. Brenda and I did the mall thing. We had a very good time. In the middle of shopping, we ate in the food court. Talking for over an hour was much easier than I thought it would be. She and I are on a common wavelength that bonds us. I had to smile from ear to ear when her face glowed as she gave me every detail of her beautiful new granddaughter. She showed me her cellphone full of pictures.

At times my thoughts drifted off to envision Bill's face, and I only heard half of what Brenda was saying. But I'll have to pat myself on the back: I never brought up Bill's name. Not even once. I don't know how I got through the day without his name on my tongue. At times everything seemed to drag out, and I saw this mental image of a melted clock, Dali-style, with the minute hand at a standstill. Then, at those times where we were really having fun, I checked my watch to find that an hour had suddenly escaped my attention. It was a day filled with mixed emotions.

When I got home and my time with Brenda had ended; the mall long forgotten, I curled up on the couch to read one of Bill's son's books. I had difficulty reading about young people meeting and testing the waters of true love. That's what I sensed, a testing of our love. Just as quickly as I focused on that mental image of us, I felt the pangs of my spiritual upbringing and tried to whisk away all thought. Maybe television would help. I turned on the news and got involved in the plight of those who are hurting. It seems the national news has nothing but agony and strife. As I felt deep compassion for those hurting souls, it helped me forget my own agony for the moment.

It's almost time for bed. I'll have Kitty to dream with as she curls up around my toes. She's such a sweetie.

Our Angst Heightened

t's three o'clock in the morning, and I'm wide awake. The only thing I want to do is sit on the edge of my bed and write in this diary. It's been a few days since I made an entry, and I'm anxious to put down all that's happening. Kitty just got up to arch her back against my side. She's a great companion. I think of her as another human who can understand me. I confide in her often, talking to her about my love for Bill and the determination I have to make certain I keep my moral fiber strong.

She's pushed her way against my thigh to share the comfortable mattress. She's already closing her eyes and trying to sleep. My wish is for a decent night's sleep as well, but it just isn't happening. I'm emotionally as high as a kite, with extreme urges that refuse to let me sleep. The image of Bill's crooked smile and his dancing eyes won't allow me to get any rest. Instead, I toss and turn and ache for him. We've been really conscious about putting ourselves in precarious situations that may lead us to become too involved. I mean *too* involved at this juncture in our relationship. At least that's what I've focused on as we spend time together. Him ... well, he's all testosterone, and sometimes that fact overwhelms me.

We had an explosive day at the beach, and right now I'm trying to clear my revved-up mind. When I use the term *explosive* I mean that it was mind blowing for me. He wore a nice pair of powder-blue trunks that accentuated his deep tan. Even at his age, he's well-built and looks great in a bathing suit. Of course, he complimented me, as he always does. I wore my wide-brimmed straw hat, some decorative sunglasses, and I was outfitted in my dark pink (almost raspberry) one-piece swimwear. He admired my long legs. I secretly appreciated the workouts I get on the treadmill. My legs are taut and shapely. I'll have to admit, they look really good for an old gal.

Our day on Sand Key Beach was more like another picnic. We had lunch and took in the sun. Later we dipped in the warm Gulf water. Bill warned me that we shouldn't go out more than a few feet. "Sharks have been on the move very near the beach," he whispered.

"Why are you whispering?"

He scanned the beachgoers and then added in a soft tone, "Don't want to cause a panic. People have been known to lose a leg in shallow waters."

After that scare I frowned at him and tiptoed back to the hard-packed sand. He followed. "I didn't mean to alarm you," he said. "I only want to protect you from any and all danger." His smile turned to a leer and he added. "Gotta protect those beautiful legs."

He was so sweet, so kind, and so shielding. Bill thinks of every little thing that I need or want, and he provides it even before I can consider that I need it. We eased our way up the firm sand until we got to the white dusty stuff, where our toes flipped through loose white sand. It was tougher walking, but we finally made it to where our beach towel was spread. We plopped down into beach chairs under a large umbrella. He picked up a crossword puzzle book and began. He's the only one I know who does them in ink. That amazes me. Either he is that sure of his ability to complete them without error, or he does them light enough to mark over each misstep. In any case, Bill is something very different from the men I've known. While he quietly put the answers in the proper spaces, I read articles in *Southern Living*. Every once in a while, I'd glance over at him and think about how comfortable it was just to be with him at the beach. We seemed to be so perfectly matched. We didn't talk much, and that was fine with both of us. Just being together was so satisfying that we didn't need to openly converse.

My brain captures those little things he's done, and it replays them again and again. For instance, he touched me about a week ago. It was a very intimate gesture, something more in line with how a husband would care for his wife. [Now that's a thought I didn't imagine before I actually wrote it.] Anyway, we'd been shopping and stopped by Hardee's for lunch. I got one of their delicious, hot ham-and-cheese sandwiches. We sat in the car and ate. Even though I had placed napkins in my lap a bit of the cheese dripped on my slacks. He stopped me from wiping it off with a napkin and took his index finger and swept it up. I tried to hand him the napkin but he waved it away and licked the yellow cheese off his finger. His smile was so naughty that I blushed. "Gooood," he drawled with eyes closed as though to savor the flavor. After that he dipped the paper napkin in a cup of water and slowly rubbed the stain away from my slacks. It was his left hand holding my leg near the knee that was so tender and intimate. That warm hand on my lower thigh got to me. I've played that moment over so many times that I believe I've added to it and just don't realize how much. Maybe the way I recall it now isn't what really happened at all. I think he pushed his fingers into my leg to secure my slacks to it, but to me it was more than that. Funny how we all want certain moments to be much more than they are. It's like fishermen who tell stories of the one that got away: the fish grows with every telling. Maybe my recollection of his hand on my leg has grown out of proportion to what really took place. I recollect that the cool, wet water from the napkin added to the sensation. When he was through the stain was almost out, but not quite. He said I'd have to treat it with a stain remover before I washed it in order to remove it completely. Then he took out his handkerchief and patted it dry.

As I recall it at this moment a sigh makes me slump a little, and I'm looking down at Kitty. She's asleep against that very thigh Bill touched. I've got to stop thinking like this. Even Kitty brings me mental images of Bill. She loves to push her way against me and make certain we're together. It reminds me of how I feel when I'm with Bill. I want to worm my way close to him, closer than I should at times. There I go again, always equating everything and every instance with my relationship with him. This is madness.

I've decided I have to lie down and at least try to sleep. As I check the clock again, I see that only a few minutes have passed. But at last I feel tired and think I can get some rest. I'm going to put this journal aside and give sleep a chance.

This morning I'm in agony. Today would have been my anniversary with Frank. Here I am in love with another man a little over four months after Frank's death. I don't understand how this happened. I have a friend who says that God has a plan for every life. He works His plan and allows us to make decisions to follow that plan or not.

If we follow it, He blesses our decision and does things secretly that make life very good. When His plan works in us, we find ourselves in situations that seem to have happened mysteriously; almost by accident. My friend may be right, because that's exactly what has happened to me. My plans had been to live as a caregiver's counselor to those who were going through the trauma of living with an Alzheimer's or dementia patient. My job would be counseling and nurturing them back into normalcy. Now that I reflect on it, how could I nurture anyone? That couldn't have been God's plan. I'm the one who needs to be counseled and encouraged back to normalcy. What brought me to this place in life? Love, romance, and a future with a man like Bill were so far from my original concepts that I had steeled myself against the idea. But God! Here I am experiencing the love of a man who … well, I'll go ahead and say it, who makes me feel like a real woman: a vibrant, desirable woman, yes, even an extremely loveable woman. He doesn't see the wrinkles, the splotchy skin, and my waning memory. Bill wants me just as I am. And I want him.

Lord, am I wrong? Should I feel like this? Have I displeased You with my desire for this man? What am I to do? Again, I need Your answers so badly that I feel lost. I'm like a little girl who doesn't know where her mother is. In this case, she doesn't know where her Heavenly Father is. Where are you, Lord? Where are you?

The agony I'm experiencing has to do with the fact that one minute I'm dreaming that impossible dream of life with Bill, and the next instant I'm in deep depression over his failure to believe in God. Without *that* we have nothing. I'm being tossed like a ball on turbulent waters.

Bill and I talked last night, and he said he had a bad day. It was my fault. Well, maybe not. But in order to protect his male ego, I'll take the blame. It started that morning when he called, and I told him I was hurt.

He asked, "Why? What happened?"

I blurted, "You won't be in church with me on Sunday. That hurts me. You at my side in the service would make life perfect." I guess I was, in fact, trying to shove it down his throat. Or had I reverted to feminine manipulation again? This is so complicated.

I hadn't realized how much my declaration bothered him. It wasn't that he wouldn't be in church. That didn't bother him as much as the fact that he had hurt me by his refusal to go. From what he told me, my anguish tore at his heart. He said he had written a long letter to me pouring out his thoughts.

I asked, "Will you read it to me?"

He read his letter over the phone. Among his writings was his hope that we had resolved the "religion issue." One of his problems is that he doesn't understand why God would allow certain terrible things to happen to people. He's a sensitive man.

I said, "Bill, when an alcoholic dies of liver disease, whose fault is it?"

He was silent.

At least he didn't hang up. He's open to discussion, even if it is one-sided.

I answered for him. "It's not God's fault. We make our own choices. We have a free will. Because of our sinful nature, we make wrong choices that lead us to destruction."

He injected, "It just seems that if God is all-knowing and all-powerful, He could, and would, stop all that."

I addressed that issue. "If the Lord did take full control and stopped all the bad things we humans are prone to get into, we would be robots programmed to do everything

His way. Instead, he made us humans who have a choice to have it our way or His."

He didn't seem to hear me and added, "I have such a problem with religion. I can't believe there's a Creator of all this and that He's watching us struggle with disease and poverty and everything that's wrong with this world. Do you realize that over half of the world's population has no clean water? That's outrageous! Where is your God in that?"

I took a deep breath and silently prayed for wisdom. "You want to be satisfied by first having proof of God. Instead, God says, have faith, and then I'll prove myself to you."

I heard him sigh before he answered. "That's my point. It's all backward."

"No! No, it's not. What you're trying to do is understand the Creator of all life from the viewpoint of a created being. It's like an ant attempting to understand an elephant, or a little boy trying to understand why his father won't let him play in the street where his ball bounces better."

Bill shook his head. "I don't see how life is relevant to any need for belief in a Creator."

"You know, Bill, Billy Graham's daughter, Ruth Graham Lotz, said it well when she was interviewed. She said, 'We need to trust that God has a greater purpose.' That's the key. We don't have all the answers. We can't see into the future. I think we value our own opinions so much that we don't give God a chance to prove Himself to us. So, what's wrong may not be all that wrong in the light of what's to come. Please listen. May we forget what's *wrong* and focus on what's so amazing about our existence?"

"What do you mean?"

"Well," I began, "have you ever noticed that all the parts of your body have different functions and each part is made to meet that function for the good of the entire body? All the working parts of the human body that work together to make us who we are couldn't have just fallen into place. Nor could they have evolved to become so perfectly meshed and fine-tuned. The reason I say that is, if just one of the elements gets out of balance for a long period of time, the human body rejects it and we die. Evolving into this perfection can't have just happened. Take a look at the preciseness with which we're formed. I mean, notice that the palm of your hand has a different type of skin than the back of your hand. The palm has a definite print, and the back grows hair follicles. Have you ever stared at your hand and tried to figure out where the back stops and the palm begins? The blend is so perfect that it's just about impossible to see where one type of skin leaves off and the other starts. Notice, too, the palm doesn't have the ability to grow hair because God created it that way. Another thing is that you have taste buds on your tongue. No other part of the body has the skin structure your tongue has. Yet even with those taste buds, you can't taste anything unless you're able to breathe and allow your sense of smell to amplify those tastes. The proof is: hold your nose and try to taste what's on your tongue. You can't taste it. Remember your mother making you take medicine as a little boy? When it tasted awful, she said, "Billy, hold your nose, and you won't taste it." With that fact alone, God is showing us that the many parts of our body have to depend on other parts in order to work to their full potential. Again, to evolve to this state is impossible, because the body won't function properly if it's less than this final stage of perfection. So, there's no way we could've been less than fully developed when we were created. Notice, too, the strong acids in your stomach and intestines don't eat out the linings of those organs, yet they destroy any other type of flesh that you eat and make it conform to its purpose, giving off nutritional value. What is that? It's God's mechanism for digestion. Bill, all you have to do is use your practical side and see that everything is so delicately balanced that there has to be a Creator and Overseer of every part of this wonderful existence. You've told me how practical you are, so I'm at a loss to understand why you don't use that practical nature to see God in all this. Let me tell you that God has not left us alone to wander aimlessly through life. He's brought balance into it so that we're able to make a choice. Just as Adam and Eve had the opportunity to choose good or evil, we have the choice to honor God or to deny Him. It's up to you, and it's up to me." I paused to take a breath, not having any idea I would make such a speech.

He grabbed the opportunity. "But religion has thousands of variations. Which religion is right?"

"Bill, I'm not into religion, I'm into *faith in Jesus Christ*. It's about a relationship not a set of religious programs or ideals. Because of what Jesus did, dying to atone for my sins and bringing me into a right relationship with His Father, I have faith in God for the direction of my life. Sometimes my natural inclinations deter His direction. Even so, He allows me to make the choice to either serve Him or serve my own wants. And don't overlook the fact that no other system of religion works on faith alone to make things right with God. All those so-called religions have duties to supplement any faith they may espouse. They have to work to become better and better in order to attain what some call nirvana. Many of the religions have idols, statues, and some even worship mountains. But, Bill, what is a statue? It's something born out of the human mind and then formed by human hands. Now, why would anyone want to worship something that some other person conceived of or who even said, 'This star fell from heaven, and it's our god.' It becomes ridiculous as you analyze it. But Christianity has forgiveness for our failures and attainment to the higher level of life wrapped up in what Jesus Christ did on the cross. All a person needs is faith in that single act that God orchestrated for our salvation."

His next words nearly brought me to tears.

He said, "If our difference in belief is that much of a problem for you, we may need to stop seeing each other, or go back to being just friends."

I took a deep breath. "Is that what you want?"

Several seconds passed before he softly admitted, "No, not at all."

I doubted, at that point, that we could really go back to being *just friends*. Our romance had grown into much more than that. We had come to the point of no return.

He continued with, "But what do you want? Do you feel we've come to an impasse?"

When he said that, the thought of not seeing him again overwhelmed my emotions, and I felt drops of moisture trying to surface behind my eyes. But I held back and muttered, "I don't know what to do." There was silence from Bill's end of the phone.

In my mind I questioned, *Why God? Why this stress point? Are You in this moment as well? Are You trying to show me something that is valuable for our relationship?* Immediately those verses came to mind that say we must "give thanks in everything and for all things." *But, Lord, how can I thank You for Bill's lack of faith?*

Bill interrupted my thoughts, "I'm at a loss too. If we go on, you'll be denying your faith. If we stop seeing each other, we'll both live in agony."

I asked, "Are you willing to give it another month?"

"We can try it. If that's what you want."

"Do you want to stop seeing me?"

I immediately prayed, *Oh, Lord, don't let him say he wants us to quit seeing each other.*

He laughed into the phone. "I think I already answered that question. In fact, that's not even a question that needs an answer."

"I need to hear it," I said. "I need to know exactly how you feel."

He was slow to bring out the words, but finally did. "Lilly, you have taken me to the very mountaintop of life's best. I never want to go back to the valley. You're so different from anyone I've ever been close to that ..." He sighed. "Well, I'll just say that Mary and I were God doubters at best and God haters at worst. When she got sick, I didn't even consider God, either as the One who put this on her, or the One who could heal her. But now, I have a reason to live. I don't know if it's the faith you have or simply your divine personality. All I know is that I've found you and never want to let go."

I melted.

After we hung up, I remembered the apostle Paul's admonition when he said he thought it was all right for a widow to seek a new husband, but it had to be "in the Lord." Again I was perplexed, and I prayed more fervently than ever. Paul's admonition also included his idea that he thought a woman would be better to remain unmarried. My head spun, and once more I took issue with the great apostle.

As I consider Bill's words, I sense a crack in his thick armor. I hope I'm not hearing what isn't really there.

Oh, God! Help!

Since I just awakened to face this new day, I'm amazed. Usually it takes me a good cup of coffee and some time to wake up fully. This morning is different. As soon as my feet touched the carpet I was wide awake, and I grabbed the pen and pad to write. As I recall last night, I remember my eyes growing heavy as I slipped into that realm of dreaminess that clouds reality, and Bill and I were teenagers again. Like a couple of kids, we were out to conquer the world and all its ills. We vowed that we could do it as long as we were together. As young adults, the problems we humans face are nothing compared to our youthful romance. At least that's the way it was when I had my first "true love."

Another thing that concerns me is the fact that I never had children of my own, and I always wanted a family. I was a career woman before I met Frank, and when we married I was on that cusp where pregnancy is iffy. Now I thought, if Bill and I were to marry, I would have his daughter and son and their children; an entire family to love, and to accept their love. But I agonized over my feelings of self-doubt. Could they love me and make me part of their family circle? After all, Bill and Mary were married for half a century, and the children and grandchildren may consider me an interloper. Marriage at my age? Is it out of the question?

As I wrote, my inner self was agonizing.

God, where are you?

Just before I wrote the sentence above, I must have had some sort of physical reaction, because Kitty was suddenly agitated and pushed against me and meowed several times. I petted her and tried to be rational. The harder I attempt to think calmly, the more the mental gymnastics play havoc with my feelings.

I know in my deepest being that I'm able to bring

happiness into Bill's life and that he has what it takes to make me very happy. But I'm still agonizing over his lack of faith. There's that niggling little spot in the back of my brain that wonders if I'd be able to live out my love for Jesus as Bill's wife. I mean, I've always considered myself a strong Christian, but am I? Can I really follow the dictates of my heart and be married to a man who isn't sure God even exists? I feel the tension gripping my mind. What will I do?

I'm going to lay the pad aside to fluff the pillow. Kitty is still curled up where she's been laying with me. It's time for me to go into the kitchen, get my coffee and head to the back porch for some serious meditation about God's will for my life. I'm going to search the Bible and look to Him for answers.

Our Fulfilling Love

everal days have passed since I even considered an entry into my recollections. A lot has happened that kept me busy. I'm ready to put the memories of my week into this treasure of recollections.

Not long ago, Bill and I had that serious conversation that said we'd give our relationship another month to see what would take place. Well, it appears we're both going overboard in an attempt to make it work. He's been more than I could have ever asked in a man. As I've stated many times in this diary, he's always been very good from day one. But after our conversation about possibly going our separate ways, he's pulled out all the stops, and the tune he's playing is beyond my comprehension.

Before I write anything else, I have to state emphatically, *I'm in love with William Harper Carrington!* I just stopped to look at those words. I cringe. Even with that love statement printed on the paper, I continue to wrestle with my spiritual side of this commitment. Maybe I feel that it's the lack of spiritual commitment that bothers me. No! No, the lack of it isn't really true. I'm as committed to the Lord as I've ever been. However, I'm tossed back and forth as I consider this physical love interest and the warmth and excitement Bill brings into my life. He stimulates me in so many ways. I feel like a new woman. Bill brings out the best of femininity in me. He seems to add that missing part to my existence. I have to keep reminding myself that Frank was ill for many years, and as a caregiver I received nothing from him, no love, no affectionate snuggles, not even words of encouragement. Now I've been blessed with all of it. The elements are there telling me that Bill was sent by God. Then I ask myself if God would send a non-Christian into my life to woo me and please my mind. Would God allow my emotional being to be satisfied by a man who doesn't believe in Him? What about Bill's potential for fulfilling my physical desires? Would God put such temptation in my life? The Bible tells me God is not the tempter nor is He able to be tempted. So, how did Bill come into my world? That's my real problem. If God didn't send him, who did? Or is this just one of those right-time/right-place things that seem to be a part of life?

Here's a thought that came whizzing through my mind and zapped me. Years ago, I was in the office of a very fine Christian minister when I noticed a three-by-five card thumbtacked to the wall behind his desk. As we talked, I focused on that card. I suppose that it was merely a reminder to him each day as he came into the office, and it spoke volumes to me. Printed on it was a simple statement of fact and faith:

> GOD, IF IT'S ALL RIGHT WITH YOU,
> IT'S ALL RIGHT WITH ME.

Why would that thought invade my mind right now? Is the Lord telling me everything is all right with Him? Is He trying to relieve me of this burden of ... *guilt*? Oh, I hate that word. It isn't that I feel guilty; *uncertain* would be the more appropriate description of my emotional state. I'm fighting with myself over the idea that God would use a man who doesn't even believe in Him to give me my heart's desires. I mean, come on here. This flies in the face of everything I've been taught. Maybe that's why I'm so uncertain. Maybe what I've been taught about God isn't really how God is. Didn't Paul even say in First Corinthians that he was writing about widows and marriage on his own? He said it was him talking, not the Lord, when he said a woman should marry "in the Lord." He also added that it is "better if she remains unwed." How many times am I going to cover this ground? I've dug it up for the third time. Why? Because it's plaguing me. I don't think remaining unmarried is the answer; especially for me. Hashing it over again is pointless unless the Holy Spirit gives me some revelation concerning my own life, not Paul's views. It reminds me that after my initial encounter with Jesus, I'm supposed to work out my own salvation with fear and trembling. I'm working at it while tightly gripping my faith-hold on what Christ did for me on the cross. That thought makes me feel like I'm going out there on a precarious branch. I'm still questioning everything.

Is God using Bill to fulfill my need for companionship, even for love? It seems so. Yet I've always heard that God doesn't use ungodly people to satisfy the desires of the godly. Does He? Immediately upon that declaration I was reminded of Proverbs 13:22, that tells me that God uses the wealth of the ungodly to give to the godly. That concept is backed up in Ecclesiastes 2:26. So, He does use those who don't have a relationship with Him to fulfill the desires of those who do know Him. Can we put God in a specific box and just say that's how God works in every situation? I don't think that's right at all. But we have to see what the Bible teaches on any given subject and make our lives conform to what that teaching gives us.

I wish I had truly studied the scriptures so I could go back to the original texts and understand the Hebrew and Greek words. I guess some people, when they see my doctrinal outlook, will scoff. Even so, it seems to me that there are so many facets and nuances for each circumstance that God has millions of ways to work out the particulars. But I try so hard to understand the Creator of the universe with my finite mind.

I've read the book of Acts and I've always amazed to find that the Holy Spirit prevented the apostles from going to Asia to preach the gospel. Now who would answer the question correctly if asked, "Who might prevent the gospel from being preached?" Most people would attribute that to the enemy of our souls. But in this case it was God's precious Holy Spirit. God is not the author of confusion, so the confusion I may feel about all this is of my own making. I'm trying too hard to comprehend every aspect of God Almighty, when I have a tough time trying to understand how the sun doesn't burn up.

I'm having difficulty understanding what happened last evening at our Bible study. Pastor was teaching us the family line of Christ. He used the first chapter of Matthew to go through the various people involved with the genetic heritage of our Savior. When he got to "Salmon fathered Boaz of Rahab and Boaz fathered Obed by Ruth," I was floored. Although I had read the lineage of Christ before, I hadn't noticed that it was by a prostitute that Boaz was birthed and put into the heritage of the Lord. That made me think of how Rahab the prostitute hid the spies from

Israel's enemy so that they could escape detection and thus report back to Joshua. The promise to her was that she and her family would be spared when Israel's army came to destroy Jericho.

I feel God giving me a glimpse into His perspective of life on planet earth. He used a prostitute (a condemned woman of the streets) who apparently was married to Salmon, to birth the great-grandfather of King David, a man after God's own heart. Is God trying to tell me that my perception of Him is wrong and that He's the author and moderator of this romance I'm experiencing?

I'll admit, my thoughts are a jumble. One minute I feel clear headed, and the next I'm wondering if I'm thinking right at all. Oh, I don't even know what I think. In fact, I don't think I ever knew what I truly believed about how God works out His plans for our lives. All I ever thought was that He does God things that we humans are incapable of understanding what, how, when, where, and why. Now, more than ever, I cling to that concept. We are finite and He is infinite. How can we possibly understand such extraordinary thinking? I have believed that God always answers prayers for righteous and godly people. Yet when I now look at certain biblical passages, I find that He has used the ungodly to bring about His plan. Then I muse, *Surely He wouldn't use a man like Bill to work out His plans for my life. Would He?* There I go again. If anyone is wishy-washy, it's me. I don't know what to believe.

Oh, Lord, now what are you doing to me? If this is a test ... What?

This is either the most coincidental happening I've ever encountered, or God is showing me something very special about His will for my life. And of course He's changing my view of Him and the methods He uses to bring about His will. Is this new perspective of Him an integral part of my spiritual growth? I sure hope so. I wish there was someone I could talk to and get feedback from. As they say, "That ain't happenin'." I don't know anyone who would be able to understand and clear up the confusion I'm experiencing: not in my church or my circle of friends.

The days are so jumbled. One day appears to speed by so fast I feel left behind, then the next day drags like a snail on his day off, and I get very anxious.

At Bible study this week I almost felt like God was toying with me. Reverend Hassler seemed a bit distant. Not that he was uncaring or unloving, rather he appeared to be in a realm of the spiritual world that is rarely visited; the class never seemed to catch up to where he was. Maybe he just caught us all off guard. It happened just after the opening prayer. Pastor said, "Before we get into our lesson tonight, I have a statement and a question." He scanned the congregation and said, "Some of you don't understand what God does to make His plans work. You don't comprehend just how He's able to put certain people in your life in order to create circumstances that work out His will for your good." He smiled as he continued. "Yes," he said with resolve, "He's working out His will for your good. Remember Jeremiah 29:11?"

Again he let it sink in, before going on.

"Let's take a quick peek at what God is up to in His Word." Then he hesitated and added, "Before we do that, I want to pose a question for all of you to ponder." He asked, "Who prevents the gospel from being preached to those needing salvation through Jesus Christ? Is it the devil? An evil spirit? Or, the Holy Spirit?"

I couldn't believe that he'd bring up the very concept I'd entered in this journal just a week or so prior to this class. It was amazing. I knew the answer. Of course, the consensus of the entire class said the Holy Spirit would never prevent the gospel from being preached. I didn't voice my understanding of the scripture reference and just sat back and listened. Yes, I'll admit I probably had a Cheshire cat grin on my face because I had read the account and knew what was coming.

The pastor had the widest smile. He went on to explain that God has plans, an agenda that He wants to take place in His time, and He will use the means He knows will work to make certain His agenda is fulfilled. That's when the pastor asked everyone to turn to Acts 16. He read from verse one through verse seven. After that he pointed out the words in verse 6, "since the Holy Spirit did not let them preach the Good News."

He scanned the congregation. "Uh, oh! It seems that, in this case, it was the Holy Spirit who prevented the gospel from being preached to this group of people." He waved his right hand at the open Bible poised in his left hand. "This passage has shed new light on just how God works out His plans. He doesn't necessarily use the people, places, and things we think He *should* use or *would* use."

Maybe it was my imagination, but Pastor appeared to glance at me. Instantly, I was uneasy and wanted to get under my chair.

He continued. "And we all have God figured out— at least we think we do. But God won't use the tools of human thinking. Remember He says, 'My thoughts are not your thoughts, nor My ways your ways.' God admits that He is a paradox. He goes on in that passage to tell us that we can't even attain to His thoughts or ways. So, why do we try so desperately to understand the Infinite when we are merely finite? Why do we not simply have the faith of a little child?" He lifted an eyebrow as he scanned his listeners. "We need to let go of our traditional thinking and put our trust in God. Are we going to mess up at times? Sure, we are. Is God going to dismiss us as unworthy because of these mishaps? Absolutely not! How do I know that? Because He tells us He knows our frame, and that we are made of dust. And Jesus made it very clear that He would neither leave us nor forsake us."

Pastor explained that God's agenda included a trip for Paul and Silas. They were to go over to Macedonia, which is now part of Europe. But they thought they should go into Asia. That's where they planned to go. We can see that the Holy Spirit prevented them from going *where they wanted to go* in order for Paul and Silas to preach where God wanted them to preach." He scanned the congregation again and added, "Sometimes God does things in our lives that seem out of character with our preconceived ideas about Him. In fact, at times we misinterpret various passages to fit our doctrinal concepts. We attempt to twist God into our mold instead of yielding to His plans for our lives.

"Notice that after they got to their appointed destination, God also allowed them to be beaten and thrown into prison. In the eyes of many Christians, that's out of character with God, and they'd question whether these two men were really led by the Holy Spirit. But we need to hear the words of Jesus in the ninth chapter of Acts. The Lord tells Ananias that Saul of Tarsus was scheduled to learn about the 'great things he must suffer for my name's sake.' That leads us to understand that being a Christian isn't always a bed of thornless roses. Sometimes God takes us into the valley of the shadow of death in order to bring us out on the other side for His greater purpose. While we're going through that valley, we have to trust that He is [as He says] with us."

Whew! This was some deep stuff. My eyes were open to a whole new concept, and my pastor was reinforcing what I now saw as the truth. God uses means we don't consider God-like to perform His will. As I thought about God the Father sending His Holy Spirit to stop the truth from being preached in Asia at that time, I was taken aback by it. But now, after reading the full account and seeing what Paul and Silas did with the jailer and his family, and the preaching they did in that region, where a seller of purple, Lydia, also came to the knowledge of the truth, I can see that God was right (of course) to divert them to Macedonia. *Imagine that.*

Now I'm thinking some weird stuff as I segue from this new concept of God into *my* world. I'm asking if God would bring Bill into my life and allow me to have a hunger for and an unbelievable physical attraction to this man in order to fulfill His purpose? What is that purpose? Is He working on Bill to make him a believer? Or, is the Lord working on me to ... to do what? Sure, as with any Christian, I have areas that need work, but I don't see how bringing Bill into my life would shore up the areas that need improvement. Just writing that statement made me realize that what I think needs improvement may not be what God sees as lacking. This is getting a bit weird; too much for my pea brain. I have to admit that my sensitivity to His will has been heightened since I met Bill—like sandpaper on the tips of a safecracker's fingers. Whoa! Did I just see how His will is working through Bill's existence and closeness to me? So, Bill is my human sandpaper. All right, I'll give Him that one. I'm taking a long look back on that hospice evening meeting and how my latent desires came alive when Bill came through the door. As I think about it, I have to admit that my spiritual nature also sat up and took notice. It's the old question, *which came first, the chicken or the egg?* Did my passionate nature rise up first and then my spiritual nature follow? Or did my spiritual nature stand up first because the Holy Spirit inside of me sensed I would need to be fortified against my natural inclinations? Is that what God saw in me that needed work? Did He see that I was weak when it came to my need for close human contact of the masculine kind; and that my spiritual self would give in to my physical, mental, and emotional desires? This is getting too deep for me. I'm just a woman who loves God. I'm not some super Bible scholar. All I want is to understand what God wants of me.

Oh, Lord, where are You? What are You doing to me?

Nine days have passed since I made an entry into this steamy diary. I've reread the last couple of entries, and I'm still confused. The mirror of my soul reflects a woman who is desperately struggling against sin—or at least the strong desire toward sin—in order to please God. But that same woman rationalizes her feelings for this unspiritual man so that she can, at least, tempt her baser instincts. That's heavy stuff. Hard to admit. I feel pushed down into a tight space. In fact, as I retrace my life since we first met, I'm like a whipped puppy. I'm curled up in a corner asking God to rescue me, yet I see the opportunity to run and play and enjoy life with this man of my dreams. I'm no better off today than I was nine days ago. I'm still fighting with myself.

What began as friendship has become passion like two very young and eager lovers. But what it may be is the coming together of two mature people who desperately, unceasingly pursue romance at every turn. The touches, kisses, and warm hugs make my life a mountain of whipped cream with the cherry on top. Now that's funny. I guess I'm giddy and school-girlish because I have never written such drivel. But that's how Bill makes me feel— above the ills of life. When I'm with him I'm no longer part of the Medicare groupies. My AARP card isn't valid when he's around—I'm free and young, a desirable *yin*!

The turning point of our relationship began just seven days ago. I'll never forget October 19, less than five full months from the day we met. We had a dinner date at the Pepper Mill. We both love that secluded little table we always get. It's our table set apart for our time together. Holding hands across the tablecloth and gazing into each other's eyes, speaking the language of romance without even a word is so much a part of living now.

When I look at him with the candlelight dancing off his sparkling eyes I'm taken back to a time when drugs, illicit sex, and all this violence didn't overwhelm our culture. It was a time of safety and freedom. The police were respected and protected. America has lost so much. Even so, Bill gives me that feeling of security once again. When I'm with him I'm safe and free to be me. My life has that added sense of excitement now that we're together. His touch is tender, yet so electrifying. I say that because I remember that our day began with indescribable electrical forces in the air. It was easy to discern that we both felt the positive tension when he called. The powerful energy that permeated the atmosphere was all around me. It radiated through the receiver. He had whispered into the phone many times before, but not like he did that morning. His voice was husky and the words very sensual. "I want you, my darling. I want to sense every part of you. To become one with you. To caress you in ways you never dreamed possible."

My legs grew rubbery and I could feel the heat of his words creating impulses deep within me. Then, just as softly as he had spoken those words, he transformed them into an easy way of hanging up. "I'll pick you up at four," he breathed. "Please be ready?"

I promised I would.

After putting the receiver on the hook, I mused over "being ready." The intonation and double entendre had me spinning toward emotional ecstasy. The Song of Solomon trickled across my mind in splashes of sensuality.

I had to discuss my feelings with God.

Lord, you know how I think. You allowed your servant, Solomon, to write it out so that I wouldn't feel that this experience was less than ... what? I don't know. I'm confused.

Again, I'm asking myself, *less than what?* Less than His best for me? Even with that, I felt that God was not unhappy with the way I yearned for Bill.

Lord, Your Word is clear. You made male and female to complement one another.

Am I now rationalizing? Oh, the ache within me.

I went into the bathroom to ready my shower. After turning the water on, I eased into the bedroom and stripped. I looked at myself in the dresser mirror and eyed the old lady staring back at me. I checked the sagging skin, the wrinkles and the gray hair. A grunt heaved my shoulders and I smiled at myself. "You're blessed," I said.

My Bible was on the dresser. I opened it and searched

out the Song of Solomon. I could feel my lips stretching into a smile of understanding as I read, "Your feet are beautiful in sandals, you daughter of a prince. Your round thighs are like jewels shaped by an artist." I checked myself. Round thighs? Yep, I'll give myself that one. Maybe a little more rounded than I needed. My eyes went back to my reading. "Your navel is like a round drinking cup always filled with wine. Your stomach is like a pile of wheat surrounded with lilies." I took the Bible into the bathroom and glanced into the brightly lit mirror there. That's the problem with the bathroom mirror; it's too brightly lit. Unlike the bedroom mirror, the one in the bathroom shows so much more of the flaws. I sighed. "It is what it is," I admitted.

The description out of this book of the Bible was so graphic. I went on reading. "Your breasts are like two fawns, like twins of a gazelle. Your neck is like an ivory tower. Your eyes are like the pools in Heshbon near the gate of Bath Rabbim. Your nose is like the mountain of Lebanon that looks down on Damascus. Your head is like Mount Carmel, and your hair is like purple cloth, the king is captured in its folds. You are beautiful and pleasant, my love, you are full of delights. You are tall like a palm tree, and your breasts are like its bunches of fruit."

I stopped reading and peered at my image. I'm tall compared to the average American woman. When I checked out the rest of my figure the smile on my face made me shake my head at my breasts. "Pretty small bunches," I said as I eyed them. I laughed out loud. Bill's reference to "the exotic" was a take-off of the Song of Solomon, and he didn't even know it.

I read on. "I said, 'I will climb up the palm tree and take hold of its fruit.' Let your breasts be like bunches of grapes, the smell of your breath like apples, and your mouth like the best wine."

I paused to check my image again. The shower was hot and steaming up the mirror. As I scanned the misty image from the top of my head to my knees, I said, "*Lord, You've given both male and female to enjoy each other. This powerful magnet within my being is pulling me to him. He too wants to partake of the exotic fruit of my body. And, Lord, I have to be honest with You; I want him to take me, make love to me, and carry me away into bliss.*" I swallowed hard. "*But, Lord, I don't want to disappoint You. What am I to do?*"

As I stepped into the shower mixed emotions filled me like never before. Hearing my declarations aloud in my own voice rattled me. Yet the need for love gripped me and dragged me into a cloud of pink that encapsulated me, and all I could think about was Bill's body next to mine. I caught a moan escaping my lips. My mind raced. Sex has never been at the top of my relational list. Oh, Frank and I were very active when we were young. But as the years passed, we were less and less prone to engage in intimacy. Because of that, when Alzheimer's hit and romance took our sexual expression to the pit and buried it, I barely noticed. Now, though, my sensual stimuli came from every angle. It seemed that everything about Bill created desire in me. I was going haywire in my old age. In the middle of a deep sigh I muttered, "*Help, Lord. Help.*" I paused to listen to my inner voice. All I could hear was the thump of my heart. I showered quickly and toweled off.

The day couldn't fly by fast enough. Seeing him dominated my every thought, and the hours dragged toward that moment when he came to sweep me away. As I look back on it, there was something strange going on that kept me from thinking of spiritual matters. I was locked onto what was taking place with my bodily need for fulfillment. Oh dear! What am I saying here? I'm writing as though I didn't know Jesus as my personal Savior and the Lord of my life. What I now look back on and recall reminds me of some ... some ... woman like the woman described in Proverbs 7. But she was a married woman who was enticing a foolish young man. I'm a mature widow in love with a mature widower. I'm not some prostitute or adulterous female.

The deepest breath I believe I've ever taken just heaved in my chest. There has never been such a struggle within me from the first day of my Christian experience.

Well, I guess I'll go ahead and enter what really took place that day and how I felt at that time. I've been very candid thus far, and I'll continue to be open with my notes. So here goes.

When he arrived around four o'clock, he seemed to be in a hurry to get out of the house and back into the car. After the way the evening went, I now know why. I too was in a rush to go eat and get it over so we could return to the house.

As we drove through the early evening neither of us said much. Again, as I recall it, I see us sitting in that front seat staring out the windshield, leaning forward, squinting into the light rain. It was as though we needed to get to the Pepper Mill, eat and get out as fast as possible.

He wheeled the car in and parked where he usually did.

The restaurant was aglow with candlelight and soft background music.

Wait a minute. I just read what I wrote. I don't remember the Pepper Mill having background music. Am I losing touch with reality? Did we even go to the Pepper Mill? Yes. Sure, we did. It's all so cloudy. Does Bill have me in such a tizzy that I can't separate my love dream from reality? Is my recollection skewed to the point that I am losing touch with the moment? Do I now hear music of which no one else is aware?

I have to stop writing about that night right now and pray.

Lord, what's happening to me? Am I living under some sort of spell? Do I even believe in spells? Have I been drugged with a potent, underlying love potion? I need to hear from you, Father. Help me make truthful entries into this diary so that no one reading it after my death will doubt what happened. My hope is that You receive glory from the way I live my life. I'm only human. Please help me as I write.

After sitting back, I took another deep breath. Now I think I'm able to go on.

I have no idea how we actually pulled ourselves away from one another to eat our meal, but somehow we did. Whether the food was good or not made little difference to us, and we finished and left. It seemed that the light Florida evening rain was there to make the moment more sensual. There I go again. Look, I've come to the point of writing about lust in just about every paragraph of my diary. It's ridiculous. This isn't a godly journal any longer. It's a steamy adult autobiography that reminds me of one of those sleazy paperbacks that filthy men used to buy in the backroom of pool halls back in Prohibition days. (I'm not that old, but saw it in the movies.) This is far from who I am. My love affair with the Lord has always taken precedence over any other relationship. But the last several months have me failing to get down to business with God. My prayer life has suffered greatly. Or has it? I pray more. But even that doesn't belie the fact that I'm thinking more about Bill than I am about God. I'm forever putting off my Bible reading and morning prayers because thoughts of Bill overwhelm my mind. Many times, as I read God's Word, I find myself having to read paragraphs, even chapters, over again because I read superficially. I somehow read the words but don't take them into my consciousness, because the thoughts of Bill override all other brain processes. That's the oddest thing about the human brain. I can read, not comprehend, and have ongoing processing of Bill and me at the same time. Then, I come to myself and realize I've read paragraphs and haven't gotten one thing out of what was read. Then I can go back and clear my mind of thinking of us and focus on my Bible reading and get back into it with ease. We are fearfully and wonderfully made, indeed.

So, as I consider it, my wondering thoughts may have hindered me at times that I was unaware. I may not be reading the Bible with clarity, but I'm actually praying much more. In fact, I'm praying all the time. But it's not the kind that most Christians think of as prayer time. There's no stopping and getting into a place where I can be alone with God. My prayers are more a constant soul scream. Wow! That's something that just hit the paper without my considering the depth of its meaning. But that's what's happening, my soul is screaming up to heaven for answers. I'm desperate for help to overcome my lustful cravings. Little gasps deep within me cry out to God. As one pastor's wife put it, I'm *praying on the hoof.* Is such praying effective? It has to be, because my soul is screaming out from the deepest parts of my being, and God looks on the inside of me my heart. Not the one in my chest. That's just a muscle. My real heart is that deepest part of my consciousness.

Lord, please forgive me for this entire jumble in my brain. Something has me entangled in its web, and I can't seem to overcome the intensity of this drive. I want to get back to my wonderful relationship with You, Father. Help me, please!

Well, at least I can put the rest of this entry in and feel good about the final outcome. Maybe I don't feel as good as I should, as I recall the events of the night. I guess I allowed myself the indulgence of Bill's passion when I should have put a halt to it from the onset. I'm getting ahead of myself again. I'll backtrack.

As I remember it, after we quickly ate our meal, there was a slight drizzle when we left the restaurant and went to the parking lot. Bill opened the car door for me, and I slid into the seat. He bent down with droplets of rain trickling along his face. He hesitated, then leaned in and gave me one of the most passionate kisses I've ever received. Maybe it was the wetness of his lips, with the taste of fresh rain mixed into the flavor of him. In any case, it set me on fire. That's when I should've stopped myself, sat back and did some heavy praying. But I was intoxicated with the wine of his kisses. There was something in me that needed to be dealt with, and I was unwilling to confront it. I'll admit I pushed it way back, somewhere beyond any rational thinking. I wanted so much to be ravished by his kisses and romanced into that pink cloud of ecstasy that I buried every righteous and godly thing in me. Why? Why did I do that? Why didn't I take control of the situation from the onset? I wish I had the answer to that.

My goodness! I just read what I wrote in that last paragraph. In fact, I've reread it four times, and each time the recall of that wet kiss has me reeling again. That's why I didn't take control, I was staggering too much. I was out of control; drunk with love. Look at me. I'm thinking like two very different people. On one side I'm supposed to be this dedicated Christian woman who wants her relationship with Jesus to be genuine and solid, built upon that Rock of my faith. The other side of me is acting like that adulterous woman of the streets described in Proverbs. I want him to have me and I want to have him. This is tearing me apart. I also want God to be alive and pure in my life. And I want to be alive and pure for Bill. I feel like I'm losing touch with reality.

Let me think out why I'm writing all this narrative. My initial purpose was because I thought it was therapeutic. Now that I look at it, I wonder if that's true. Is it therapeutic or is it a way of reliving every sensual instance? I just took a deep breath so I can relax and consider everything that I felt during those exotic moments. I'm smiling because that's exactly what I'm doing: reliving each second so that I can experience the ecstasy all over again. Talk about honesty. That's as honest as I can get.

I just glanced at the clock. This is so odd. Between this moment and the words written above that say, "Let me think out why ...," six minutes went by, and I was totally unaware of it. I'm sitting here, ostensibly to write in this diary so I have a record of what's happened in the last several days or weeks or months. However, each time I write a paragraph I go into some sort of reverie and stare off into space while I relive the various moments. The warmth of each touch, each glance, and each tender kiss brings back a veritable slideshow of my love dream. What's going on with me? I'm captured in Bill's grasp. Or is it *Bill's* grasp? Can it be that I'm enslaved by some deep, hidden lust of the flesh that has always been a part of me? Were Freud and Jung right? Have I now allowed the sensual side of my id the indulgence it desires? If so, why now? If so, why with Bill? If so, why has it taken this long to rise up and make itself known?

Lord, I'm so full of questions and so void of answers.

My body is racked with deep sighing. I have to take

a few moments to recover. I'll get a glass of iced tea and get back to writing out my feelings. I'll continue to take a look at my struggle with God and my battle with myself.

Okay, I have that refreshing tea, and now I'll get back to my recall of earlier that evening. I'm being honest with God, with myself, and with the fact that I believe everyone struggles with secrets. I'll continue to reveal my secret desires and go on as openly as I am able.

It seemed that it only took moments to drive from the parking lot at the restaurant to my place. I don't even remember unlocking the door and Bill and I entering the house before we were sitting on the sofa holding each other. Something different was stirring in me. I sensed that Bill felt it too. It was as though we both had the urge to consummate our relationship this very evening, and neither of us could do anything about it.

Our kisses were more passionate, deeper, fuller, and stronger. Just holding each other wasn't enough, and we began clutching, grabbing, and pulling at each other's clothing. I've seen such passion portrayed in scripted movies, but never, ever dreamed it could actually happen to me. I have to continually remind myself that we're senior citizens. We're supposed to be past this stage of life. What is this? My only answer is: *a love dream*. Sometimes it feels more like a nightmare of mega-spiritual proportions. Is that what this is—spiritual warfare?

God, where are You?

As I recall, we were seated on the sofa. I noticed Kitty out of the corner of my eye. Bill was unaware of anything. He was busy nibbling on my neck. However, my cat was trying to jump up on the sofa and worm her way between us. At that instant the passion pulled me into ecstasy and I could only think to sweep her away with my left arm so the moment wouldn't be missed.

Primal instincts rose to a crescendo, and our love exploded into the longing to become one in body. It's so difficult to explain my feelings without sounding like a child who has discovered all the toys under the Christmas tree are for her, but I'll try.

My feelings that were hidden for so long broke through the surface, gasped for the fresh fragrance of love, and, with abandon, plunged deeper still. I wanted desperately to give way to my passions. I was like a lioness in heat. Fulfillment was all that was on my mind.

Kitty again jumped up on the sofa and arched her back against me. I gasped, awakened from my trance of passion. I instantly stiffened against Bill's touch. My cat actually stopped me from making that last move that would have united Bill and me. If it hadn't been for Kitty, we would have been together, truly together. My arms were around him, but instead of pulling him to me I loosened my hold. He was so tender, gentle, and caring. This was the moment we had both been waiting for. His breath was hot against my neck and his body moist as he hovered over me.

I slipped my arms down and put my hands on his chest and applied minimal resistance. His shirt was moist with perspiration. "We can't," I whispered. I pressed a little harder and felt him ease his focus.

Kitty jumped down and went into the kitchen. Now that I look back on the moment, it seems she felt she did her job of interfering and left the room. Her services were no longer needed. It was time to go eat or drink or do what cats do after they have done the will of God.

Even though he was far from the Christian I had

always wanted, Bill was every bit the man I dreamed of. He regained his quest and eased down to nuzzle my neck. With Bill still actively pursuing me, I asked God for His forgiveness. I pushed against Bill's chest again. "This isn't going to work," I whispered. "Please understand that I'm not trying to tease you and then back off. I didn't intend for us to go this far. Please forgive me."

It was as though he suddenly awakened from a daze and pulled back. A frown tore at his brow and he looked down at me. "You don't want ...?" He didn't finish the question.

"I want you," I said. "But not until ..." I didn't finish my statement. How could I use the word *marriage* when he hasn't asked me to marry him? He hasn't even hinted at it. Maybe I'd said enough to make him realize that I wasn't about to make love without the sanctity of God's blessing. After Kitty's interruption of my passion, my decision was more an act of my will than it was of my conviction. It seemed as though my enslavement to passion was broken and I had regained a will of my own. I was suddenly able to know what was right and made the conscious decision to follow that path. Actually, as I look back on this romantic fling over the months, Kitty provided my first real act of Christian principles without me beating up on myself for doing so. God used my cat to bring me to my senses. At least that's how it appears to me.

Lord, did You make Kitty push her way into our passionate situation? Is that how You made a way of escape? I'm so happy she was there with us to stop my foolishness. I still want Bill, but now realize that I have the power to wait. If he doesn't accept that, so be it. I'm going to serve You, Lord, and that's my final answer.

Even after all that, there's a sense of wonder deep inside my mind. I'm still questioning whether the church leaders have truly taught us the proper view of sex outside of marriage. Oh, I know the verses and can't wash them away. Here I am, still fighting with myself. It's not that I want to give in and make love to Bill before we're married. I'll admit there have been moments like the one I've just described when, married or not, I was ready. Not any longer. I'm just interested in taking a deeper look into all that's said in scripture about this subject.

I'm laughing as I reread what I just declared. Now that I'm sitting here making this entry it's easy to write "Not any longer" and mean it. But when the time of passion with Bill is knocking at my mental and emotional door, I wonder how I'll respond. Will I open the door and ask him in, or will I be able to close it, lock it, and call beyond the barrier and tell him we'll have to wait? I'll let that question sit and simmer before I go wild with trying to answer it.

Now I'll get back to what happened after I stopped Bill. He gave in to my wishes, and we both sat up and straightened our clothing. I rationalized again, right there while we got ourselves together. I asked myself how this wonderful act of love for two mature humans could be wrong. Didn't we love each other? It's so natural to want to express that love in physical terms. After all, we're still in these bodies, shriveled as they are. And we continue to have feelings, desires, and more than that, we have unrelenting passions.

Bill's breath against my neck pulled me back to reality and I let myself slip into the ecstasy of his tender affection as he held me close. "I want you so much," he whispered. His lips were against my ear, and I could feel his hot breath. I was in love, and I was loved. This is more than a passionate dream. It's reality.

Our Questions

fter I had pushed him away, I don't know why I expected Bill to leave and never come back. Well, that's not quite true. I do know why I expected it. All I could think of was the way boys in high school and college use young girls to get what they want and then leave the girls so they can crow about their conquests. Or, if the girl didn't give in to the boy's urges, he would leave her for someone who was willing to give him everything he wanted. But that was in school, years ago. It was made up of teenagers and very young adults who (at least for the girls) had moral standards. It's what I remember. I know it's far different now. Even so, it's kid stuff. And it's the way I remember it.

This is not some kid. This is Bill, a mature man who has total respect and love for me. My mind won't allow me to entertain any negative concept of him. He's an honorable man, and he loves me. I have to keep telling myself that his love is pure and he has no ulterior motives from which he might prey on my vulnerability. But why do I have to keep reassuring myself? It's as if he hasn't proven to be a man of integrity. He has and I need to accept that and go on.

Something is niggling at me about what I'm writing

concerning Bill's attitude, and I can't put my finger on just what it is. I'm going to stop writing to think it through.

I took a ten-minute break, got a glass of iced tea, and considered how I feel and why I feel it. If it all sounds mixed up, it's because I am mixed up. Even so, my musings as I sip the refreshing green tea lead me in another direction. In fact, the processing of all these facts has made me consider my motives. Am I the one who's using this lovely man to meet my own need for companionship, even though God's Word says I shouldn't be unequally yoked with an unbeliever? Am I really the Christian woman I pretend to be? Have I pawned this off on God's plans for us instead of actually facing the fact that my loneliness may be the culprit? My own laugh just echoed in my ears because of the thought that ran through my brain. The thought was, *Maybe I'm a fake Christian after all.* I'm really beating myself up in order to discover the reality of where God is in all this mess. I'm coming down harder on myself than I ever have. I guess I need this emotional beat down. Facing reality as I talk to God is important, because I can't take my feelings to anyone else. Of course, I've considered Pastor Hassler, because he's a competent counselor and my shepherd—the guide for this confused ewe. I'm reluctant because this is a woman thing, and he's a man. He wouldn't or couldn't understand, so I'm mentally checking for other women in my sphere. As I visualize each one, I can see the scowl on any and all faces and dismiss each. I've continued to remind myself that none of the women I associate with would understand. That means I have to get real with me on God's terms. Ouch! That didn't even feel good. I'm held at bay with my love for the Lord, and that makes me want to unveil my deepest feelings to Him. But He already knows. Oh, woe is me. I have to make some tough decisions based on God's Word rather than on my emotional fulfillment—and that settles it. I'll have to admit it; a real war is raging in my mind. Is this the battle that the apostle Paul was writing about in the seventh chapter of the book of Romans? I'll have to go back and read all that one more time so I can get a feel for the camaraderie that links me to that great apostle.

Giving in to my primal feelings would eradicate this war, but afterward I'd feel like I had lost the battle, and the wounds would ooze with the pain of giving in to my urges. That would begin another war of contrition, my need for forgiveness and total repentance. My heart tells me that if I give in, God will understand and love me anyway. But I still want to do the right thing. Not that my giving in to Bill's desires would instantly throw me out of God's Kingdom. I'm not that Armenian in my view of God's grace and mercy. But it sure wouldn't be pleasing to Him if I just threw caution to the wind and had my fling. And isn't pleasing God what this Christian life is all about? I mean, I realize that I'm saved by grace and grace alone. However, after my salvation experience there is a compulsion to live my life in such a way that God is glorified. After all, it's all about Him. Yes, just as all of us are, I'm still under construction. So, everyone will have to pardon my dust. He set me free from my sinful nature in order for me to live a life that would be pleasing to Him. I'm not saying that pleasing Him does anything to save my soul. As I just said, that's taken care of by way of faith in the cross and the resurrection of Jesus Christ. But as a Christian, my life is not my own to fling. Is that even a proper concept?

Stopping to think it through like this is good. I'm away from Bill, and my mind is much clearer. Being in his arms gets me all fuzzy headed. In fact, even being in the same room with him has me in a whirl. I need this break in the action. Even with the time and space, I'm still questioning every aspect of this relationship. I just wish I could see into the future and know what God has in store for us. I'm laughing because I included "us" as though God has a plan for Bill and me to be together. Does He? What if He has plans for me to be alone? Then He'd let Bill go do whatever he'll do if I'm not a part of his life. If I could only read the mind of God and understand what His plans are, I think I'd be a lot saner.

As I consider it, I'm either in chronic denial by saying that Bill in my life won't hurt me, or God is onto something very different from what I've been taught.

I'm laughing because I just caught my fingers tapping on the table top. It's a habit I developed back in college. When I contemplated the answer to a question that I had no clue about, I'd tap my fingertips on the desk as I pondered. However, I'm coming to some conclusions as I work through each day and write my feelings in this journal. I'm calling it prose therapy. Let me think about that.

It's true. My concept of our relationship is rapidly evolving into rational considerations. I mean, I'm very happy with Bill, but I'm thinking through those times with him and asking myself if it's all as real as I hope it is. And of course, I keep asking myself if God is in it. When I go back to that very first moment I saw him, all the way forward to what almost took place between us on my sofa, I have to really twist and turn to find anything that's not perfect. The only change I might wish for would be to get him to commit to the Lord very early in our association—before love set in on both of us. I realize that a woman doesn't marry a non-Christian in hopes of changing him. The funny thing is, I didn't plan any of this, and I believe it's the Lord Himself who has created the circumstances. Just last week our minister spoke at length on Jeremiah 29:11. *I know the plans I have for you, says the Lord, plans for good and not for evil, to give you a future and a hope.* I've got to go with that. I mean, I've got to believe that God has plans for my life and that He knows exactly what He's doing. Since Bill just appeared at that meeting, and since there was no other seat available for him, and since we struck a melodious chord from the beginning, I have to conclude that one of God's plans for my life was for those elements of this relationship to take place. I know one thing. God's Word promises to give us the desires of our heart when we search for a committed relationship with Him and pray earnestly. Well, Bill couldn't be a better fit for that image in my heart. I believe Bill is God's answer to my yearning soul. So, that answers how *my* needs are fulfilled, but what about Bill's needs? He doesn't even know that he needs a real and lasting relationship with the Lord Jesus. How does that play out?

He thinks in terms of the essentials of his *earthly* wants, needs, and desires. Of course, since he isn't a Christian, he can't think any other way. Does that mean God is handing me the job of living the life in front of Bill in order to get him to make a commitment to Christ? Oh my, am I in trouble, or what? I wonder how many single women in our large church would want to take on such a daunting task. I know that God knows what He's doing, but I sure don't know what He's up to. I feel so ill-quipped for something so important. Immediately I remember there is a verse that tells me that when I'm weak, that's when God is strongest through me. I sure hope so.

I love what Reverend Hassler said when speaking on the subject of God's plans for each of us. He said, "God is never caught off guard. He has never once scanned the earth and all that is taking place and put His hand over His mouth in horror, gasped, and declared, 'I didn't know that was going to happen!'" Everyone in the congregation laughed. He waited a moment for his audience to calm down and added, "We may think our lives are out of whack, but He promises to be with us. He has it all under His control. He's working out the details of every aspect of His plans for our lives so that there'll be no question that He's in control."

Of course, what our Pastor said gives me comfort because I know it's the absolute truth. Even so, when I look at the close-up of my life I see chaos. However, when I step back and try to see the entire picture through God's perspective, I get a feeling that all is calm. Hmm. Am I trying to rationalize again? Maybe not. Let me consider it on paper.

God knows all of it and is directing it as well. Therefore, the Lord wouldn't put Bill in my life and set up the potential for marriage and the commitment that goes with it if He couldn't see a future for me with this man. I have to take that and run with it and believe God is going to draw Bill to His Son, Jesus Christ. That's another thing I learned recently. I always thought it was the Holy Spirit who draws people to God, but our minister pointed out John 6:44 and 6:65, where Jesus said, "No one can come to me unless the Father draws him to me." What a revelation that is. It's changed the way I pray for people. It's revolutionized the way I pray for Bill. And it's cleared up what Jesus told His disciples when He told them not to ask Him for anything anymore, but "ask the Father in my name." That really makes sense now. Wow! I just realized how much closer to God I've come since Bill has materialized in my life. This internal wrestling match has produced a yearning to know God better.

It seems I'm on a spiritual rollercoaster ride. The highs are exhilarating, but the lows plunge me into the depths of despair. I have no control of what's taking place. *Oh, Lord, help me.*

I believe I'm going to come to a conclusion here. I've thought it out and this is what I believe is right. I think.

The final word is that I believe Bill is everything I hoped for. I believe God is in this relationship. Most of all I believe that the Father is drawing Bill to a real and lasting relationship with His Son. That leads me to ask more questions, but it also finalizes my belief concerning this phase of my life.

Unfortunately, that leads me to ask, what about sex before marriage? Isn't the Bible clear on the subject? But are we dealing with widows and widowers who have been living under the marriage covenant, been sexually active, and are now free due to the death of their spouse? Are we free to pursue the fulfillment of our natural inclinations? If I give in to my fleshly cries to have union with Bill, will I lose out on heaven? I don't think so. However, I've been doing some real studying lately, and in Paul's letter to the Philippians he tells them (that includes me) to *be careful to do only those things that are pleasing to God.* I have to "fight the good fight of faith." I mean, I can't succumb to my fleshly yearnings. I know that the three basic sins are the lust of the flesh, lust of the eye, and pride of life. I feel like I'm preaching to myself. Why? Because I'm afraid the next time I'm with Bill I won't have Kitty around to get in the way, and I'll fail to resist his persistent kisses. The thought zapped into my mind: *Don't put yourself in that situation.* That's so easy to say at this moment. But when reality hits and Bill and I are together, the physical attraction is powerful and unrelenting. That situation seems to just slip up on us. We don't plan it. In fact, it seems so natural for us to want to be in union.

A very odd thought hit me. When are two people who are in love actually married in the eyes of God? Is it when that preacher or justice of the peace says, "I now pronounce you husband and wife"? Or, is it when the commitment to be partners for life happens in the hearts of that couple? I'm getting too deep for my own good here. I'm certain theologians would all have varying opinions on that one. It seems like some of this modern thinking is rubbing off on me, and I'm trying to superimpose the new normal into my own situation. As I go back into the Old Testament, or even into the transition gospels with Joseph and Mary and the Eastern thinking of that time, I find marriage to be a gray area. Vows meant lasting commitment. The vow to marry was as good as the act of marriage. I have to take a very deep breath. This fight within me is too much to handle.

I'm going back to look at those three basic sins. I've been taught that all other sins stem from any one or a combination of those three. How is God looking at me now? I'm so close to giving in and having a full-fledged affair with Bill that I've already done it all in my heart. I'm laughing, because I just remembered that former President, Jimmy Carter confessed to a writer for *Playboy Magazine* to having lusted in his heart. Have I done that which is so forbidden that I'm going to mess up my relationship with the Almighty? I'm reeling with questions, and I'm emotionally staggering as I grasp at what seems to be answers. My one sure answer is: *I—don't—know.* I'm certain I didn't need to write that. Anyone reading this journal can see that I don't know anything about anything when it comes to this relationship.

I keep thinking that maybe I shouldn't be writing and baring my heart like this. I'm plagued with the thought that when I'm gone and someone discovers this diary, they'll judge me harshly because I've given in to my sensual urges before I marry this man. Even though I haven't yet taken our relationship to that point, I'm still afraid of my weakness and the prospect that I will give in. My mental picture is of someone reading this and saying, "Since she's aware of her potential for giving in to complete the sexual act before marriage, why doesn't she just flee?" That's a valid point and one I need to address. Maybe the best way to address it is to ask anyone who may read this diary: have you ever been conscious of the potential for sin, even argued with the Spirit about what's before you, but you plunged ahead anyway? I know women who have passed along gossip and then told me after the fact that they "shouldn't have told" me or anyone else. They were under the conviction of sin but wagged their tongue anyway. I need to consider that I'm starved for affection. It would be impossible for me to turn away from what I crave. Yet God's power is at work in me to want and to do His will. I'm going to fight the good fight of faith and keep myself right before God. However, if I fail ... well, if I fail, and Bill and I have a sexual liaison before marriage, then I'll fall on my face before God and beg His forgiveness. However, I'm going to give resisting my best shot.

My fervent hope for people who may read this journal is that they will consider their particular plight and then check their spiritual mirror. The song that says, "Put your hand in the hand of the Man who stilled the waters," goes on to say, "Take a look at yourself and you will look at others differently." Staring into a spiritual mirror and seeing the spiritual reality of myself isn't something I relish. It's a hard fight to be real with my own shortcomings.

Don't we all have battles that seem to take us to the wire? Haven't we all given in to certain urges? Then we shouldn't judge each other too harshly. What we sow concerning the way we treat others will be exactly what we reap. Unless I'm mistaken, all sin is sin. There are no big sins and little sins. Lying is just as sinful as adultery. Doesn't it say in the book of Revelation, "and all liars shall have their place in the lake of fire"? We all need to be careful about judging too quickly and too harshly. We need to stop lying to ourselves.

I feel like the apostle Paul when he argued with himself and asked, "Am I out of my mind?" I put it another way. I ask myself why I sink to arguing with myself. That's easy to answer. It's because I'm trying to convince myself that what I'm considering is all right. Even righteous. Why righteous? Well, if the outcome is that we marry and that Bill finally comes to a saving knowledge of Jesus Christ, isn't that a noble cause for which I may be deemed righteous? (I'm smirking right now, because I know I'm blowing smoke in an attempt to justify myself. The end never justifies the means if the means is not right and pure.)

But who am I to be talking about marriage? Bill hasn't said a word or hinted at it to this day. It's been six months. I guess it's a woman thing again. We all want those great male/female relationships to culminate in marriage. At least that's generally true about women in my age group. Sure, Bill may walk away if I don't give in to these urges we both have. But I don't think he will. As odd as it may seem, I sense God in all I'm thinking and doing. As I already stated and want to say again, God has plans for me. God also has plans for Bill. I believe one aspect of His plans is for us to be together. There, I've said it, and I'm convinced of it. *I think.*

My fears that Bill might have wanted to taste the fruit of my body and then walk away are relieved. He's proven to be the man I knew he was. With all the tenderness he has displayed since I met him, this wonderful man still treats me like a piece of fine china. Even though I stopped the lovemaking process before it took place, and even though I allowed us to get hot and heavy on the sofa but refused to take it all the way, he continues to treat me with deep affection and total respect. His caring touch, his voice so soft, and his consideration of my feelings in every aspect are more than I could wish for. Wow! He'll make a wonderful Christian.

Puzzling Moments

t's almost impossible to believe that it's been three weeks since I made an entry into this diary. I've been overwhelmed with going places and staying up at all hours with Bill. We've played board games, watched two wonderful movies, and sat together as he did crossword puzzles while I read one of Joyce Meyer's fantastic teaching books.

No, the romance hasn't died down. Not even a little bit. It's more like we take breaks from kissing, hugging, and peering into each other's eyes. Within a couple of hours, we're back at it again. We just can't get enough of each other. I'll have to admit we came so close to making love several times during these three weeks that I'm ashamed of it. No, not because I gave in and we actually completed the act. We didn't. Rather, just putting ourselves into that situation where anything could have happened if we had just one more kiss, one more caress, one more of those sexy looks. Each time we were on the verge I floated into a cloud of ecstasy. At times we have exhausted ourselves and have fallen asleep on the sofa. We've dreamed together.

Today I learned more about Bill. He even loves to shop with me. He's not like those men who go shopping with their wives, only to get in the mall and sit on a bench with their cronies and let the women shop alone. In fact, we went to Countryside Mall today, and he was right at my side in every store. He even encouraged me to try on shoes, dresses, and pantsuits. He sat outside the dressing area, and when I pranced out to dazzle him with my latest find, he'd give an honest and sweet appraisal. One thing I noticed that is so special about Bill is that he absorbs the tiniest fact about me and stores it away for future use. An example is the fact that pink is my color. I've never had a color chart done. I just know that pink is me. I don't know when Bill discovered that fact. But one thing is certain, he uses that bit of information to help me select the right clothing and shoes to fit my best color appeal.

When we passed the well-known lingerie shop's window display, he commented about the scantily dressed mannequin not holding a candle to me. I was genuinely embarrassed. "It's true," he assured me. "You're still so young and vibrant, so full of life. You sparkle with radiance that's unmatched by any woman, no matter her age or figure." He took my arm and turned me to him. People were passing by. Some of them were very close. He didn't appear to notice anyone in the mall but me. "You're the woman every man dreams he will meet some day. And," he continued with a slight smile, "you've chosen to spend time with me. I'm so blessed."

I thought, *Did he really say he was* blessed? *Was my Christian lingo rubbing off on him?*

I put my fingertips on his mouth. "Shhh," I said. "If you keep on, we'll both be openly crying right here in the mall. What'll people think? I mean what will Victoria's people think?"

We laughed, and the solemn moment passed. Even so, my heart was filled with hope for the future. I was floating down the west wing with Bill at my side. Life was so meaningful that I wanted to lift my hands toward heaven and shout praises to God. But Bill had my hand in his, and we were swinging them as we walked. I mused, *Just a couple of kids, totally in love.*

This is funny. I just stopped writing in this diary to consider that word *love*. I've written about us being in love and that we're totally in love, but as I attempt to recall it, I don't believe we've ever actually uttered those words to each other. This is so strange. I'm racing through my recall trying to think back on a moment when we were kissing, hugging, or even on the verge of making love that either of us actually said, "I love you." I can't bring it up. Am I just forgetting in my old age, or have we skipped one of the essential elements in communication between lovers? We hold hands, we hug, we kiss, we utter sweet words to each other, and Bill has offered some of the most poetic phrases that say he loves me, yet those three words have never been strung together and pointedly spoken by Bill, or by me. Isn't that strange?

Even so, I'm sure of his love for me, and there's no doubt that I'm deeply in love with him. I know we've expressed our love through many other channels. Yes, the words are nice, but the actions speak so much louder and are far more important. I just sighed, because I see that I'm trying to kid myself again. Those three words are the most important three words on planet earth. And I just attempted to downplay them when, in fact, I want to hear them from him and I want to express them to him. I've decided to do just that. As I determined to do so, I immediately balked because a woman never initiates the romance and never, ever is first to say "I love you." I can't help it. That old-school teaching keeps surfacing.

Funny, but we're always clinging to each other in public. It's as though each of us wants to show the world that we're in love. He opens the car door for me, always walks on the street side of the sidewalk, and never misses an opportunity to help me step off the curb. What a gentleman.

After a particularly fun shopping day, Bill said, "How about a picnic tomorrow?"

I was delighted. "Sure."

"Would a return to Taylor Park be all right?"

"You're not going to throw me to the alligators, are you?"

He laughed. "No. I promise I'll restrain myself."

I kissed him right there in the parking lot. "I love you!" I blurted. I didn't mean to say it. It just tumbled out. However, as I look back on it, I still consider the kiss and my declaration as another act of feminine manipulation. I didn't intend to force him to say anything. But the picture of my arms flung around his neck; with me planting a kiss on his lips, and then my joyous outburst of my love for him, left no room for the poor guy to maneuver. That's manipulation at its finest, or worst.

He didn't respond as I looked deep into his eyes. Instead, he held my face in his gaze and had an odd expression. No doubt about it, I had him cornered.

I asked, "What are you thinking?" *Ouch! Was I pushing him deeper into the corner?*

Tenderness in his gaze melted me even more. He reached up and put his palm on my cheek. "I was just thinking ... ah, well, that I guess there has to be somebody, like a god, who is directing all this."

I tightened my grip on him. "Oh, Bill!" I shouted. "There isn't 'a god,' but there is *the* God who created the world and is watching over it all. He even has plans for us."

Bill took in a very deep breath. "We'll see," he said. "Tomorrow will tell the tale."

I could feel my brow pull together. "What on earth are you talking about?"

"You'll see." He smiled. "Tomorrow we'll check it out at Taylor Park."

I nodded. Our second date, almost seven months ago, was a picnic at Taylor Park. Now the weather was a bit chilly, even in west-central Florida. I determined to dress for the weather and have a wonderful time.

I'm now sitting up in bed. I've tried to sleep but can't. All I can think of is Bill's mysterious statement about tomorrow telling the tale about God. How could a picnic at the little lake park tell us anything about what God has planned for us? I'm so curious that I tossed and turned as I tried to close my eyes and get the sleep I need. Instead, I sat up to pray. After a short prayer I got up and grabbed this journal so I could keep track of how I feel and what I feel.

Lord, I don't even know what to write any more. I'm so confused. Please do something to change this circumstance. Either draw Bill to a relationship with Your Son, or make something happen to separate us.

I don't know why I wrote that. If something happened and we did go our separate ways, I'd want to lie down and die. I'd be worse off than I was that evening just before Bill walked into the meeting room. I've got to endure for the night. Now that was odd. When I just wrote about enduring for the night, the verse came to mind that basically uses those very words and adds something about "joy coming in the morning."

Lord, is that You? Are You giving me some insight

about what to expect tomorrow? Will I experience the joy I've longed for when we have our picnic at the park? Now I really can't sleep. My eyes are wide open. Kitty is napping on my bed. She looks so comfortable all curled up. I too want to sleep, but I'm looking forward to the joy that morning will bring, and my eyes won't close.

Our Final Picnic

 'm glad I waited to make this entry. I had to have time to filter all that happened at Taylor Park so that I could come out of an unbelievable pink cloud.

I did get to sleep and slept well. When I awakened at seven o'clock that next morning, I turned on the Weather Channel while I waited to hear from Bill. His call came with his cheerful greeting. "Good morning, sweetie. It's a beautiful day, and I feel great. How are you this morning?"

"I don't think I could feel any better," I chirped. "The weatherman says it's supposed to be in the mid-seventies today."

"Good. Are you ready to have lunch on the grounds at the park?" he asked.

"What do you want me to bring?"

He chuckled. "Just like the first time we had our picnic, bring your beautiful self and that's enough."

"Are you sure? I'd like to bring something sweet to add to the picnic."

"Honey, if you brought anything as sweet as you are I'd have diabetes."

"Aw, that's over the top. Can't I bring something?"

"Not a thing."

"I can't believe this. Are you absolutely positive?"

"I'm sure. Here's the menu. Coleslaw, ham and cheese

sandwiches, pickles, olives, chips, and a bottle of extra fine sparkling grape juice. Well, extra fine isn't quite the word for it. It has a metal twist-off cap and it cost me a whopping two-forty-nine. I pulled together only the best for my sweetheart on this special day."

We both laughed as we hung up.

I stopped for a moment and looked at the phone. I wondered what he meant by "special day." Did he have something in mind that would make it special? There I go, making something out of nothing. That's why I call myself Wonder Woman. I'm forever wondering, and my mind is always wandering into areas that ... well, that shouldn't even be part of my thinking. So, I've concluded, of course it's special, it's another day we can be together. It'll revive fond memories of our first picnic. I had to smile as I considered it.

Even though he was bringing everything, I decided to whip up some dessert. That's the least I could do. Both Bill and I are chocoholics, and we can't seem to get enough of the stuff. I put together my best chocolate dream pie. It is chocolate cheese cake, with sour cream and whipped topping blended into it to make it smoother and creamier than usual. After it sets in the refrigerator, I add chocolate bark shavings on top, and that gives it a professionally created look. A thin slice of lime snipped and twisted and placed in the middle of a dollop of whipped topping adds the finishing touch that makes it so hard to resist. Because we were going to be outside, I knew it would work best to freeze it. When I completed the dessert, I looked at it before slipping it into the freezer. I felt the broadest smile as I cooed over the delicious look of it. I mused, "Bill Carrington, this will put you in the palm of my hands."

It was a beautiful, warm autumn day. The sky was crystal clear, and the Florida sun beat down to make the afternoon comfortable. The grass was never so green, and the palm trees stood stately along the water's edge. Since we were eating on a large blanket, Bill insisted that we picnic near one of the park benches. "So we can keep our food high and away from the ants and other bugs," he said. "It appears it's going to be a mild season, and we'll have to contend with those pesky creatures who want to share our lunch."

Placing the food on the bench was reasonable. As we laid out our feast and got ready to eat, Bill stopped me. "Will you say grace?" he asked.

I always did ask God to bless our food, even in restaurants, but it had been my initiative that got the job done. Up to that moment Bill had never asked me to pray. Yet he had been reverent toward my times with God, bowing his head and even in the restaurant atmosphere softly saying, "Amen."

I took a deep breath and asked God to bless our day together, bless the food for our nourishment, and give us the opportunity to see Him in our relationship. Even as I prayed that part about Him in our relationship, I wondered why I added it. I never had before. I heard Bill punctuate it with his louder-than-usual "Amen," and we fixed our paper plates and ate.

Even though Bill was his fun-loving self, something was in the air. It was a feeling I couldn't quite put my finger on, but I knew this was a very different day. That word "special" he had used during our phone conversation came to mind. Maybe it was my imagination. Then there was the fact that he asked me to pray over the meal. That in itself caused me to wonder. Even so, I had that feeling. Link that together with the fact that he recently said he was blessed, and it all made me think that a pattern was forming. I wondered if Bill was coming around to embrace a life of faith, or was he playing the game so I would feel comfortable. He had said that this picnic would answer the question about God. That thought made my head spin.

As we ate, he talked about Mary and their early years, recalling how they had married on his birthday in February. She was seventeen, and he was twenty-two. They had met when she was just fourteen. She was the youngest sister of one of his fishing buddies.

Although Mary was young and strong, she had two miscarriages before birthing Shelly. With the help of Bill's sister, the young couple purchased a small home in East Detroit.

To me, the atmosphere and the conversation covering his initial meeting and marriage seemed a little strained. He was rambling with no apparent direction or end in sight. Then the conversation took a really strange turn when he asked me to tell him about how Frank and I had met and what took place when Frank proposed to me. We had discussed this before, but not in detail. Now, though, Bill wanted all the little nuances of what took place. Even though I felt like this was already furrowed ground I sank the spade in and dug it up again. I told him about Frank's proposal to me at my office with the attorneys and other employees within earshot. He had placed his hip on the corner of my desk and leaned down and said, "How 'bout you and me get married?" That was it. It may have been a line out of a Humphrey Bogart movie. It wasn't very romantic, but it got the job done, and within weeks Frank and I were married. I told Bill how we had to move my things into Frank's apartment piecemeal. We weren't poor, but he had opened his accounting practice and hadn't built up enough clientele to pay the office rent and a secretary, so I had to chip in each month for the first year of our marriage. It was well worth it in the end.

Bill kept injecting various questions that kept the ball rolling until we finished eating. The ham and cheese sandwiches were tasty and the extra fine sparkling grape juice was superb. We laughed about the $2.49-a-bottle juice. Bill said, "I guess neither you and Frank nor Mary and I could have afforded such an extravagance back then."

I reminded him, "You know $2.49 was a day's wages back in those years."

We chuckled as we agreed that when we were young we were able to endure so much in order to make sure our blossoming love would last. We finished the last few chips as we both recalled those times when money was tight and love was grand. I had to think, *Money isn't tight anymore, but love is still grand.* I shook the thought to focus on my offering to this wonderful picnic.

I took the foil off the chocolate dream pie. It had thawed to perfection.

Bill's eyes widened. "When you said you made some dessert, I had no idea it would be something like this!" He was genuinely amazed.

I cut a slice for him and a smaller piece for me. The pleasure on his face as he slid the creamy texture into his mouth was all the thanks I needed. He closed his eyes. I could see that he allowed his tongue to feel the smooth chocolate. As he swallowed, he moaned. I knew I had made the perfect dessert. That old saying ran through my mind. "The way to a man's heart is through his stomach." It appeared I won over the stomach.

Lord, please send that same feeling to his heart.

Bill admitted that he would love another piece, but he added, "I'd better not. Let's save it for later in the day." He glanced down at his stomach and quipped, "I'm putting on some pounds since we've been dating. My doctor says my weight gain is good for me."

After we gathered the plates and jars and foil-wrapped all the food to be put in a large paper bag, there was a lull in the conversation and the action. It was a moment I can't describe. Again I sensed that something was in the air. Bill was in deep thought. I didn't question what he was thinking so as not to disrupt anything on his mind. Instead, I continued placing items in the bag.

It happened when I was putting the jar of olives away and he had the chip bag held out for me to take. I pulled my hand out of the brown sack and reached for the chip bag. Bill held onto it with me. "This is the last of it," he said. "I've got it."

I let go. "What will we do now?"

He patted the park bench. "Why don't you take a seat up here and let me finish this." He smiled and put the chips in the paper sack.

I eased up from my place on the blanket and sat on the park bench. I breathed deeply to catch the fragrance of the lake and surrounding flora. My gaze took in the panorama of the lake. The sun glistened off the tiny ripples. I turned back to watch Bill shake out the blanket and roll it into a neat tube. He placed the tube on the ground near my feet. Watching his methodical work fascinated me. He's one of those people who needs everything lined up and neat so he can feel he has finish the job. Oh, he's not a *neatnik* but a man who likes things in order.

After checking to see that the blanket was properly rolled and placed just right, without warning Bill knelt on the blanket, took my hand in his and said as softly and sweetly as any man ever did, "Lilly, I haven't told you this yet. I wanted to make certain of it before I said it." His eyes were filled with tenderness. "I love you." His brow rose. "Actually, I'm *in love* with you."

I could feel a chill run up my spine. My other hand covered his. Tears were on the verge, and I swallowed. The softness in his words and the love radiating through his eyes melted me. The moment stood still as I squeezed his hand in mine. "And Bill, darling, I'm in love with you," I assured him.

He took a very deep breath and added, "I've done something that may seem childish to you, but I want you to hear me out."

"What did you do?"

He reached up and put an index finger against my lips. "Please, don't say anything."

I watched as he repositioned his knees on the rolled-up blanket.

His eyes were moist. "Last night I asked your God to show me that He's real and that He has a plan for our lives, as you told me He did." Bill licked his dry lips. I could tell he was very uncomfortable revealing his intimate talk with God, but he went on. "I told Him how much I love you. And I asked Him to help me do today what I planned to do." Again he drew in a deep breath. "Lilly, I love you," he repeated. His eyes filled with tears.

There was a long moment that allowed him to gather his thoughts and work through his emotions. He bowed his head and held up a hand. "I know. I know. I've already established that fact." He raised his eyes to look into mine. "But like I said, I don't just love you. I'm in love with you." A tear trickled down one cheek, and he brushed it away. "But I want to be sure you understand the motivation in what I'm about to do." He reached into the sack where the food was stored and felt around. Within seconds he withdrew a little blue felt box.

I gasped at the sight of it. My mind raced. Was this happening? This love dream? Was it now reality? Tears welled up, and my vision was clouded. Was this about to be what I had dreamed it would be? Was he going to ...

He opened the box, and there was an exquisite diamond ring. He held the box up for me to gaze at its contents. "I'm in love with you, and I want you to marry me." He swiped the back of his hand across his face to wipe away the flow of tears. "If you'll have me, you'll make me the happiest man on earth." He held a hand up once more. "Before you answer, I have to tell you that I can't promise to know God like you do. But I can promise to be the best man, the best husband, the best sweetheart, and the best lover you've ever dreamed possible, and that I'll try to find a relationship with your God."

My mouth dropped open and I wanted to shout, *If I'll have you? Of course I'll have you!*

Here was this dear, sweet, loving, kind, caring man asking me to marry him. Here he was, down on his knees asking if I'd have him to be my husband. I was so stunned I didn't answer immediately. All I could think of was that he said he loved me. He repeated it more than once.

He stammered, "I–I asked God to help me do this. And I asked Him to ... to ..." He was crying openly. His shoulders shook, and he put his forehead on my knees.

I put my hands on his head. "Shhh, my darling." My vision was blurred, and I could feel tears running down my cheeks.

He raised his head and asked, "Will you please be my wife?"

I wiped away the tears on his cheeks. "Yes! Oh, Bill.

Yes. I love you. I'll marry you. I'll have you, my darling. I'm so in love with you." I pulled him to me and kissed his salty lips. The tears mingling between us were our expression of pure joy.

After a few minutes of hugging and kissing, he backed away and took the ring out of the box and slipped it on my finger. For a moment we both gazed at it through tears of joy. The sparkle from the beaming sun captured me. Was that sparkle a reflection of God's smile?

He laid his head on my lap, and I bent forward with my cheek on his back. We cried the happiest tears this world has ever witnessed. "Thank you, Lord," was all I could whisper. I would become Mrs. William Harper Carrington. God was in it. And Bill got the answer that got him started toward a true Christian experience.

Beginning Together

e planned our wedding for the first day of March. His daughter, Shelly, helped me with the wedding plans. We shopped for that special outfit I would wear. I finally settled on a soft peachy cream dress that allowed me to use pink accessories. I considered what was happening and nearly lost it right there in the store. I had to use their restroom just to get enough paper towels to wipe away the tears, blow my nose, and rinse off my face.

Time seemed to drag by as we handled all the preparations. It was a happy time, yet there was a lot to accomplish in order to do this right. Bill and I wanted it right in every way.

When the day arrived, it was a glorious time as the ceremony was conducted in Shelly's elegant two-story home. There were friends and family cheering us on. Bill's son wrote a wonderful tribute to the joining of hearts in the autumn of life. The gist of it was that such a union had the synergy to birth a fountain of youth. The end of his prose stated: "May the sun blush and the moon hide its face from the radiance emitted by this true love." Wow! I was awed.

After I descended the stairway to the sound of Kenny Rogers softly singing *Lady*, I joined the love of my life for the ceremony. It was an awesome time. When we were pronounced "husband and wife," we kissed. Everyone cheered.

Laughter permeated the gathering and happy conversation trickled along the poolside reception. The pink three-tiered cake was created by Bill's granddaughter, Jaclyn. When Shelly offered a toast, she explained the three tiers. "Two of the tiers represent the marriages each has experienced." She added, "The top tier, though smaller, represents the golden years left to this amazing couple."

Oh, what a wonderful reception into the family. Now I have Bill's children and grandchildren to call my own, and I'm filled with the joy of God's great love reflected in my new family.

Shelly's words branded the image of "this amazing couple" into my mind. I knew it was true. We were amazing and so blessed. Yet even on my wedding day I secretly asked God to create a new man in Bill. I wanted desperately to know that God approved of all that we were doing. My struggle with myself seemed to be a never-ending battle. However, on the other side of my mind I could feel the peace that passes all understanding guarding my heart and my mind. This was quite a faith-building experience.

This Hidden Treasure

just found this diary hidden deep in the lingerie drawer of my dresser. It's been eons since my last entry. In fact, now we are five years into our marriage. Bill has made a full commitment to the Lord. If I don't seem too enthusiastic, that's because it isn't coming through on paper. Believe me, the excitement over his conversion is here. I'm so excited I can barely write. His newfound life took place right here in our home. A dear couple from my church, Roger and Emily Thornton, came by, and we enjoyed talking. Then Roger asked Bill if he wanted to "experience the reality of Jesus tonight." It was as though God put it in Roger's heart to know that the timing was perfect. Right here in the living room, kneeling at the sofa, Bill made a profession of faith in our Lord and Savior Jesus Christ.

Roger didn't stop with that but took Bill into our pool and baptized him. That was such an awesome time. The moon was full and the clouds were sparse, so that there was a haze over the pool that made the atmosphere ethereal.

It's been three weeks since I've made that last entry into this journal. We've been to two gospel sings, a Gaither event, and Bible studies nearly every night. Bill is a sponge. He's soaking up all he's able to in order to make up for the many years without the Lord. Bill's son came to our home and served communion to us. It was a moment of sweetness of Spirit like none I've ever sensed. Bill wants to know all there is to know about Jesus. His testimony includes the fact that he had never been someone who hugged people. He declares, "Now I hug strangers." This is wonderful. He always adds, "I wish I had made this commitment to the Lord much sooner."

I sense that this journal is complete and that I'll never make another entry into it. That's fine. All I know is the Lord promised that He had plans for our lives, and one of His plans is being fulfilled in my love dream.

Epilogue

During his short time as a Christian, Bill never failed to testify that it was the way Lilly lived her Christian experience that convinced him that the Lord is alive and well and is in the soul-saving business. Her demeanor gave him a glimpse into life the way it should be lived. He never knew the battles she faced every day of their courtship.

Bill was eighty-six and Lilly was seventy-four when they married. This lovely couple had over eight glorious years together. Bill was ninety-one when Jesus became Lord of his life, and he went on to meet the Master face to face on September 25, 2004. He was ninety-five. Lilly followed a few years later.

About the Author

Lillian Bosnack, a New York City resident and model during her youthful years, loved to write and dabble with prose and poetry. Her husband, Frank, had a lucrative accounting business that he sold so they could move to Florida in their retirement years. Unfortunately, Frank suffered from Alzheimer's and passed away. Now alone, Lillian sought refuge with those who met in a Hospice caregivers counseling meeting in Clearwater, Florida. There, her life was transformed.

Printed in the United States
by Baker & Taylor Publisher Services